William

Romeo a

Adaptation and activities by **Derek Sellen**
Extra activities by **Jennifer Gascoigne**
Introduction and dossiers by **Robert Hill**
Illustrated by **Giovanni Manna**

Editors: Rebecca Raynes, Michela Bruzzo
Design and art direction: Nadia Maestri
Computer graphics: Simona Corniola
Picture research: Laura Lagomarsino

We would be happy to receive your comments and suggestions, and give you any other
information concerning our material.

www.blackcat-cideb.com

ISBN 978-88-530-0686-8   Book + audio CD/CD-ROM

Printed in Italy by Litoprint, Genoa

The CD contains an audio section (the recording of the text) and a CD-ROM section (additional fun
games and activities that practise the four skills).
– To listen to the recording, insert the CD into your CD player and it will play as normal. You can
   also listen to the recording on your computer, by opening your usual CD player program.
– If you put the CD directly into the CD-ROM drive, the software will open automatically.

SYSTEM REQUIREMENTS for CD-ROM	
PC: • Pentium III processor • Windows 98, 2000 or XP • 64 Mb RAM (128Mb RAM recommended) • 800x600 screen resolution 16 bit • 12X CD-ROM drive • Audio card with speakers or headphones	**Macintosh:** • Power PC G3 or above (G4 recommended) • Mac OS 10.1.5 • 128 Mb RAM free for the application
All the trademarks above are copyright.	

Contents

This story is recorded in full.

These symbols indicate the beginning and end of the extracts
linked to the listening activities.

William Shakespeare (1800-03) by the Romantic poet and painter William Blake (1757-1827).

Shakespeare's Life

William Shakespeare was born in 1564 in Stratford-upon-Avon, a town in central England, on or near 23 April (we are not sure of the date, but we celebrate his birthday on the 23rd). His father, John Shakespeare, made and sold gloves,[1] and was an important person in Stratford. His mother, Mary Arden, came from quite a rich family. John and Mary had eight children, but three of them died young, so the young Shakespeare grew up with four brothers and one sister.

Shakespeare went to the Grammar School in Stratford. He got quite a good education, but he left in his early teens, before finishing school. His father had problems with money at that time; perhaps he wanted him to start work. So, Shakespeare didn't go to university.

In 1582, Shakespeare married Anne Hathaway. He was 18 and she was 26. They soon had a daughter, Susanna, and in 1585 they had twins, a boy, Hamnet, and a girl, Judith. Hamnet, however, died when he was only 11.

1. **gloves** : you wear these on your hands.

We are not sure what Shakespeare did between 1585 and 1592, but we know that he was already working in London as an actor and playwright [1] in 1592. Some other playwrights didn't like him because he wasn't from a university, but Shakespeare was soon very successful. In 1594 he became a member of a company of actors called the 'Lord Chamberlain's Men', so called because their patron [2] was the Lord Chamberlain, an important person at Queen Elizabeth's court. This company became the most successful in London. It built the Globe Theatre, south of the River Thames, in 1599, and later changed its name to the 'King's Men' when James became king in 1603. Shakespeare wrote two plays a year for this company until about 1608.

Many writers of this time were poor, but Shakespeare made a lot of money both from writing and because he owned part of the theatre. He made at least £200 each year (ten times as much as a schoolteacher), and in some years he even made £500. He bought land and houses in Stratford, including one of the best houses, called New Place, which he bought in 1597. His family, who didn't move to

From **The View of London** (1650) by the Dutch map-maker Claes Jansz Visscher (1587-1652).
There was only one bridge over the Thames, called London Bridge.

1. **playwright** : a person who writes plays.
2. **patron** : a rich person who gives money to a writer, artist, musician etc.

Inside **The Globe** theatre. Spectators could stand, for just one penny, or pay more money to sit down. There was room for nearly 2,000 people.

London, stayed there. Shakespeare became rich, but he didn't buy a house for himself in London.

In his early years in London, Shakespeare wrote exciting historical dramas such as *Richard III* (about 1591) and romantic comedies such as *The Taming of the Shrew* (about 1592). From 1592 to 1594, however, the theatres in London had to close because of the plague: [1] it was dangerous for many people to be together in a small place. In these years Shakespeare wrote poetry, and began his sonnets. [2] Between 1593 and 1603 he wrote 154 sonnets. More than one hundred of them describe a friendship – sometimes difficult – with a young man, and 28 of them are about a woman who the poet both loves and hates. Perhaps the man was

---

1. **plague** : this disease killed thousands of people; it passed from person to person.
2. **sonnet** : a poem that has 14 lines.

Shakespeare's patron, the Earl [1] of Southampton, but we don't know who the woman was: she is only described as a 'dark lady'.

When the theatres opened again, Shakespeare wrote *Romeo and Juliet* (about 1595). His plays in the next five years include *A Midsummer's Night's Dream* and *The Merchant of Venice*.

Romeo and Juliet (1790-91) by Joseph Wright of Derby (1734-97). The death scene is a favourite subject with artists. Almost always a cup or bottle shows that Romeo has taken poison.

1. **Earl** : a member of a family with a high position in society.

But Shakespeare wrote his greatest plays after his company moved to the Globe Theatre in 1599. His plays in this period include *Hamlet* (about1600), *Othello* (about 1603), *King Lear* (about 1605) and *Macbeth* (about 1606).

It seems he moved back to Stratford in about 1608. His mother died that year, and the London theatres were closed again because of the plague. He only wrote one play a year now, not two. These last four plays are about family members coming together again after being apart. *The Tempest* (about 1611) was the 36th and last play that he wrote on his own; after this he only wrote two other plays with other writers.

Shakespeare died in 1616, on the same day that we think he was born, 23 April. He is buried in Holy Trinity church in Stratford.

From what people wrote about Shakespeare, it seems that he was honest, a good friend, and an amusing person to be with.

The Elizabethan Age (1558-1603)

In 1533 King Henry VIII broke away from the Catholic church in Rome because the pope didn't allow him to divorce his first wife. Henry started the Church of England, and England became a Protestant [1] country. When his Catholic daughter Mary became queen in 1553 she tried to make the country Catholic again; she even married King Philip II of Spain, the leading Catholic country in Europe. But Mary died in 1558 and Elizabeth, Henry's other daughter and a Protestant, became queen. During her reign [2] England became the leading Protestant country in Europe.

In 1588 Philip II of Spain sent an enormous fleet, [3] called the 'Armada' in Spanish, to attack England. The attack failed because of bad weather and the tactics [4] of the smaller English ships, and more than 11,000 Spanish soldiers were killed.

England became an important sea power, and began to attack Spanish ships in the Atlantic and explore the Americas. Sir Walter Raleigh (1554-1618) tried to start a colony [5] in Virginia in North America. He called it 'Virginia' because Elizabeth

1. **Protestant** : of the Christian religion, but not Catholic.
2. **reign** : period when a king or queen has power.
3. **fleet** : a group of ships.
4. **tactics** : methods used when fighting a battle
5. **colony** : a place controlled by a more powerful country

The Armada Portrait of Queen Elizabeth I (*c.* 1588) by George Gower. At top left the
Spanish Armada sails towards Britain, but at top right it is destroyed by bad weather. With her
right hand the Queen touches Virginia. Her power is also shown by her clothes and jewels.

was known as the 'Virgin Queen', meaning she wasn't married. The colony failed
– the people weren't happy there – but he brought potatoes back to England. Sir
Francis Drake (1540-96) explored more than the Americas: in 1577-80 he was the
first Englishman to sail around the world.

In this period there was a lot of activity in all the arts: architecture, painting,
music and poetry. But in drama the activity was extraordinary. There were many
playwrights, such as Christopher Marlowe (1564-93), who wrote *Doctor Faustus*,
and Shakespeare's friend Ben Jonson (1572-1637), and several others, … but
Shakespeare has become a writer who is known everywhere in the world.

1 Comprehension check

Fill in this fact file about Shakespeare. Write words or notes.

Name:	William Shakespeare
Dates:	1564 -
Place of birth:	....
Family background:	....
Education:	....
Profession:	went to London; became an actor
Professional success:	....
Marriage & family:	....
Personality:	....
His writing, in general:	....
Most famous works, in particular:	....
	....
Interesting things about his life & works:	....
	....
Interesting things about when he lived:	....
	....

2 Research

Work on your own or in pairs. Are you curious about anything in Shakespeare's life, works or times that was not in the introduction? If so, try to find out about it in books or on the Internet.

3 Writing

Who is the most famous writer that your country has produced? Does everyone agree about who it is? Work on your own or in pairs, and make a fact file for this writer. Use the same model as in activity 1.

4 Speaking

Use the fact file that you made in activity 3 to make an oral presentation about your famous writer to a visitor to your country. Point out any interesting similarities and differences with Shakespeare's life, works and times.

Before you read

1 Characters

Look at the list of characters on page 12. Who do you think the underlined pronouns in these sentences from Part One refer to? Choose A or B.

1 <u>They</u> hated <u>each other</u>.
   A ☐ the Prince and Lord Montague
   B ☐ the Montagues and the Capulets

2 "<u>I</u> hate all Montagues and I hate you!"
   A ☐ Benvolio
   B ☐ Tybalt

3 "<u>You</u> are too old to fight," said Lady Capulet.
   A ☐ Lord Capulet
   B ☐ Tybalt

4 "<u>He</u> shuts out the daylight and spends all <u>his</u> time alone in the dark."
   A ☐ Romeo
   B ☐ The Prince

5 "I love sweet Rosaline. She is beautiful, intelligent and good. But she does not love <u>me</u>."
   A ☐ Romeo
   B ☐ Benvolio

6 "Mother, <u>I</u> am too young to get married."
   A ☐ Juliet
   B ☐ Romeo

Now read and listen to Part One and check your ideas.

2 Who will die?

At the end of the play five of the characters will be dead. Which ones, do you think? Write down the names of five characters on a piece of paper. Put the piece of paper in an envelope and close it, or give it to your teacher. Check your ideas only when you have finished the whole story.

The Characters

The Prince

Juliet

Romeo

Friar Laurence

Lord Capulet

Lady Capulet

Lord Montague

Lady Montague

The Nurse

Paris

Mercutio

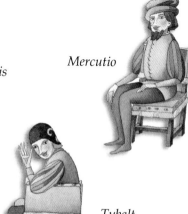

Benvolio

Tybalt

PART ONE

The Montagues and the Capulets

n the beautiful city of Verona, there were two families — the Montagues and the Capulets. They hated each other. They had hated each other for hundreds of years.

One day two servants of the house of Capulet were walking in the streets.

'If I meet any man or woman from the house of Montague, I'll push them out of the way,' said Sampson.

'No, you'll run away,' laughed his friend, Gregory.

'Don't worry about that,' said Sampson. 'I'll stand and fight.'

Just then two servants from the house of Montague came into the same street.

Sampson took out his sword [1] and bit [2] his thumb [3] at them. This was a great insult. The two groups of servants began to fight.

'The Montagues are better than the Capulets,' shouted [4] the servants of the Montagues.

'Our masters, the Capulets, are better,' shouted the servants of the Capulets.

Then Benvolio, a member of the Montague family, arrived. He tried to make peace.

'Stop, fools! [5] Put away your swords.'

But no one listened to him. The servants continued fighting and Benvolio took out his sword to stop them. Then Tybalt arrived. He was a Capulet, the most dangerous member of the family. He loved fighting.

'Benvolio, you have drawn your sword. [6] Now you must fight with me. Look at your death!'

'I am only trying to separate these fools,' replied Benvolio. 'Put away your sword or use it to help me keep the peace.'

'Peace!' snarled [7] Tybalt. 'I hate the word. I hate all Montagues and I hate you!'

With those words, Tybalt attacked Benvolio with his sword.

Then Lord and Lady Capulet arrived. Lord Capulet was old but he wanted to fight too. 'Bring me my sword!' he shouted.

'You're too old to fight,' said Lady Capulet. 'You don't need a sword. You need a crutch.' [8]

Then Lord and Lady Montague arrived. Lord Montague was swinging [9] his sword although his wife tried to stop him.

---

1. **sword** [sɔːd] :
2. **bit** : past form of 'bite' (*bite-bit-bitten*)
3. **thumb** : the largest finger; 'biting your thumb' was a great insult in this period of history.
4. **shouted** : spoke very loudly.
5. **fools** : stupid people.
6. **have drawn your sword** : (*draw-drew-drawn*) have taken out your sword.
7. **snarled** : said in an angry way.
8. **a crutch** : something to help a person with a broken leg to walk.
9. **swinging** : moving violently.

More and more people came. Soon everyone was fighting. It was very dangerous.

At last the Prince of Verona arrived. He was very angry.

'Stop fighting! I want peace in my city! Drop your weapons or you will all die! This is the third time that your families have been fighting in the streets.

'Lord Capulet and Lord Montague, you are old but you are not wise. [1] You must promise not to fight. Lord Capulet, come with me now. We must talk. Lord Montague, come and see me this afternoon. If your two families fight again, you will both die!'

Everyone went away except the Montagues. The fight was over.

'How did it begin?' Lord Montague asked Benvolio.

'The servants were fighting. I drew my sword to stop them. Then Tybalt arrived. He began fighting with me. Soon everyone was involved.' [2]

'Where is my son, Romeo? Is he safe?' asked Lady Montague.

'I saw him this morning, an hour before sunrise,' replied Benvolio. 'He was walking alone in the fields. He saw me but he didn't want my company. He went into the forest.'

Lord Montague nodded. 'People have often seen him there in the morning. He cries. Then he comes home and locks [3] himself in his room. He shuts out the daylight and spends all his time alone in the dark. Something is wrong.' [4]

'Have you questioned him?'

'Yes, but he gives no answer.'

'But look, he's coming now,' said Benvolio. 'I'll ask him about his problems.'

'I hope he will answer you. We'll leave you to speak privately,' said Lord Montague.

Romeo was on his way back from the forest to the city.

'Good morning, cousin,' said Benvolio.

'It's a sad morning,' replied Romeo.

---

1. **wise** : sensible.
2. **was involved** : was part of the fight.
3. **locks** : shuts his door with a key.
4. **wrong** : not right.

Romeo and Juliet

'Why? Why are your days sad and long?'
'I am...'
'In love?'
'Out...'
'Out of love?'
'Out of my lady's favour. I love her but she does not love me. Love is a terrible thing, Benvolio. I love and I hate. Love comes from nothing. It is heavy and light, serious and foolish,[1] hot and cold, sick[2] and healthy. Are you laughing at me?'
'No, I am sad because you are sad.'
'Love is a madness. Goodbye, cousin.'
'Tell me, who do you love?'
'I love a woman.'
'I know that. But who?'
'I love sweet Rosaline. She is beautiful, intelligent and good. But she doesn't love me.'
'Forget her. There are many other girls.'
'No, I can never forget her.'

Lord Capulet decided to have a party.
'I will invite all the important people from Verona. But not the Montagues.'

He wanted his daughter, Juliet, to meet Paris, a lord from Verona, the friend of the Prince. He hoped she would marry Paris in the future. He called for his servant.

'Here is a list of names. Go and invite the guests.'[3]

1. **foolish** : stupid (see 'fools' p. 14).
2. **sick** : ill.
3. **guests** : people invited to a party.

Romeo and Juliet

The servant met Romeo and Benvolio in the street. He did not know that they were Montagues. 'Can you help me?' he asked. 'I can't read the names on this piece of paper.'

'Look, Romeo. Rosaline will be at the party.'

'I have an idea,' said Romeo suddenly. [1]

Meanwhile, [2] Lady Capulet was talking to Juliet, her thirteen-year-old daughter. Juliet had an old nurse who looked after her. [3]

'You will meet Paris at the party,' Lady Capulet told Juliet. 'Perhaps you will marry him one day.'

'Mother, I'm too young to get married,' replied Juliet.

'I would love to see my little Juliet married,' said the Nurse. 'You will have happy days and happy nights.'

1. **suddenly** : quickly and unexpectedly.
2. **Meanwhile** : At he same time.
3. **looked after her** : took care of her.

Go back to the text

1 Comprehension check

Only ONE of the following sentences is correct. Which one is it? Rewrite the others with the right information.

1 Tybalt started the fight in the street.
2 Tybalt wanted to make peace but Benvolio wanted to fight.
3 Lord Capulet and Lord Montague were wise but they weren't old.
4 Lord Montague was worried because Romeo spent all his time with his cousin Benvolio.
5 Benvolio knew that Romeo was in love with Rosaline.
6 Paris was an important person in Verona and the Prince's cousin.
7 Lord Capulet's servant asked Romeo to help him invite the guests to the party.
8 Lord and Lady Capulet hoped Juliet would marry Paris.

2 Discussion

Work with a partner. Do you agree or disagree with these statements about some of the characters in Part One? Explain why.

1 Benvolio is Romeo's cousin and also his best friend.
2 Tybalt probably wanted to kill Benvolio in the fight.
3 Romeo has been in love many times before.
4 Juliet doesn't want to marry Paris because she doesn't like him.

3 Adjectives

A Can you remember the adjectives used in Part One? Fill in these gaps.

1 In the __ __ __ __ __ __ __ __ __ city of Verona, there were two families.
2 Tybalt was the most __ __ __ __ __ __ __ __ __ member of the Capulet family.
3 Lord Capulet was __ __ __ but he wanted to fight too.
4 The Prince was very __ __ __ __ __ .
5 'You are __ __ __ but you are not __ __ __ __ .'
6 'Where is my son Romeo? Is he __ __ __ __?' asked Lady Montague.
7 Love is a __ __ __ __ __ __ __ __ thing.
8 It is __ __ __ __ __ and __ __ __ __ __, __ __ __ __ __ __ __ and __ __ __ __ __ __ __ .
9 'Rosaline is __ __ __ __ __ __ __ __, __ __ __ __ __ __ __ __ __ __ __ and __ __ __ __ .'
10 'I will invite all the __ __ __ __ __ __ __ __ __ people from Verona. But not the Montagues.'

B   **Opposites**

Romeo uses adjectives with opposite meanings to describe love: 'Love is heavy and light, serious and foolish, hot and cold, sick and healthy.' Here are some more adjectives. Match an adjective in A with its opposite in B.

	A		B
1 beautiful		A	stupid
2 thin		B	terrible
3 hard-working		C	ugly
4 intelligent		D	safe
5 sad		E	poor
6 kind		F	lazy
7 rich		G	late
8 wonderful		H	happy
9 early		I	fat
10 dangerous		J	cruel

Why do you think Romeo uses adjectives with opposite meanings to describe love?

C   **Synonyms**

Synonyms are words which have similar meanings. For example, *unhappy* is a synonym of *sad*. Choose three synonyms from the words in the box for each of the six words in the table. Use your dictionary if necessary.

affluent   attractive   depressed   ecstatic   slim   excellent
fantastic   great   glad   handsome   joyful   miserable   pretty
prosperous   skinny   slender   unhappy   wealthy

happy	
sad	
rich	
beautiful	
wonderful	
thin	

'The Montagues are better than the Capulets.'

The Montagues are **better than** the Capulets.

In this sentence, the servants are comparing the Montagues with the Capulets.

Better is the comparative form of the adjective **good.**

We could rewrite the sentence in two different ways:

The Capulets are **worse than** the Montagues.
Or The Capulets aren't **as good as** the Montagues.

4 Comparative forms

Here are some sentences about the characters in the play. Finish the second sentence so that it means the same as the first. The second sentence is started for you.

1   Benvolio is older than Romeo.
    Romeo isn't ....
2   The Capulet servants aren't as hard working as the Montague servants.
    The Montague servants are ....
3   The Prince is richer than Lord Capulet.
    Lord Capulet isn't ....
4   Juliet isn't as pretty as Rosaline.
    Rosaline is ....
5   Romeo is slimmer than Tybalt.
    Tybalt isn't ....

'Tybalt was the most dangerous member of the family.'

Tybalt was **the most dangerous** member of the family.

This sentence means that nobody in the Capulet family is **more dangerous** than Tybalt.

the most dangerous is the superlative form of the adjective **dangerous.**

We often use phrases like in the world, in my family, in the class, I know etc. with the superlative form.

For example: Mount Everest is **the highest** mountain **in the world.**
                Bob is **the nicest** person **I know.**

5 Superlative forms

Rewrite these sentences. Use the superlative form of the adjective.

1   Nobody in my class is more intelligent than Lisa.
2   I don't know a person who is lazier than my brother.
3   Nobody in my family is kinder than my grandmother.
4   No sport in the world is better than football.
5   I don't know a place more exciting than Tokyo.

6 **Too + adjective**

Look at these two sentences from the Part One of the story.

(Lady Capulet to her husband) *'You are too old to fight.'*
(Juliet to her mother) *'I am too young to get married.'*

Make similar sentences with *too... to...* **. Use the words in lists A and B below.**
For example: *It's too late to go shopping.*

A	B
lazy	carry
tired	drive a car
fat	go shopping
young	go dancing
cold	study
ill	go to bed
unhappy	wear this dress
late	pass the test
early	go to the beach
heavy	eat dinner
stupid	learn English
poor	make a mistake
intelligent	play football

Work with a partner. Compare your sentences.

7 **Dialogues**

Complete these dialogues. Use *too* + adjective.

0   *A: Why can't you do the exercise?*
    B: Because it's too difficult.
1   **A:** Why don't you want to come swimming today?
    B: Because I'm ....
2   **A:** Shall we eat in this restaurant?
    B: No, it's ....
3   **A:** Wake up! It's time to get up.
    B: But it's only 6 o'clock! It's ....
4   **A:** Drink your tea! It's time to leave.
    B: I can't . It's ....
5   **A:** Mum! Kevin and I want to get married.
    B: You must wait. You're ....

Practise the dialogues with a partner.

8 Vocabulary – families

Complete these words. Each word is the name of a member of a family.

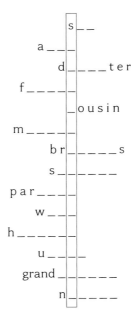

1   Romeo is Lord Montague's   s _ _

2   My father's sister is my   a _ _ _

3   Juliet is Lady Capulet's   d _ _ _ _ t e r

4   Lord Montague is Romeo's   f _ _ _ _

5   Benvolio is Romeo's   _ o u s i n

6   Lady Capulet is Juliet's   m _ _ _ _

7   Romeo is an only child. He has no   b r _ _ _ _ _ s

8   He has no   s _ _ _ _ _

9   Romeo has two   p a r _ _ _ _

10 Lady Capulet is Lord Capulet's   w _ _ _

11 He is her   h _ _ _ _ _

12 My father's brother is my   u _ _ _ _

13 My mother's mother is my   grand _ _ _ _ _

14 My sister's son is my   n _ _ _ _ _

Now read DOWN from the letter 's' in the first line. Put the letters in these spaces:

S _ _ _ - _ _ _ _ _ _ _   _ _ V _ R S

These are the words used by Shakespeare to describe Romeo and Juliet in the prologue (a kind of introduction) to his play. The first phrase means 'unlucky'.

9 Family opinions

A   Write one or two sentences about your opinions of other members of your family. Use a dictionary if necessary. For example:

I think my father is too strict sometimes.

B   Now write one or two sentences about what other members of your family think about you. Use a dictionary if necessary. For example:

My sister thinks I am too noisy.

10 Listening – The Queen of the Fairies [1]

PET

Look at the six sentences below. You will hear a conversation between Romeo and his friend Mercutio. Decide if each sentence is correct or incorrect. If it is correct, put a tick (✓) in the box under A for YES. If it is not correct, put a tick (✓) in the box under B for NO.

		A Yes	B No
1	Mercutio thinks that Romeo is deeply in love.	☐	☐
2	Romeo dreamt about Juliet last night.	☐	☐
3	Queen Mab is a real person.	☐	☐
4	Mercutio says that Queen Mab keeps us awake.	☐	☐
5	Mercutio says that Queen Mab visits girls, soldiers and lovers.	☐	☐
6	Mercutio thinks that Queen Mab is very powerful.	☐	☐

11 Now rewrite the incorrect sentences.

12 Discussion

In exercise 10 Romeo and Mercutio talk about dreams. Below is a list of things people sometimes dream about and a list of their possible meanings. Match a dream with a meaning then discuss your ideas with a partner.

DREAMS

If you dream about
1 a tree with lots of apples,
2 buying a bicycle,
3 birds that are flying away,
4 eating a cake,
5 riding an elephant,
6 ladybirds,
7 a spider sitting on you,
8 drinking fresh water,

MEANINGS

it means that
A you're not going to meet a nice person.
B you're going to have problems.
C you have many friends.
D you're going to be sad and lonely.
E you're going to have a long, healthy life.
F someone is going to visit you.
G you need to be more active and do some sport.
H you're going to have good luck.

PET **13 Writing – a letter**

Imagine that you are a 16th-century silk merchant from London. You were travelling through Verona on your way to Venice when you saw a lot of people fighting in the street. You are writing a letter to your son in England. You want to describe what happened. Explain about the Montagues and the Capulets. Describe the fight and tell him about the Prince's decision. Your letter must begin like this:

I'm writing to you from Verona, a beautiful city not far from Venice. The local wine is excellent but the people are not very peaceful. Yesterday I saw a street fight.

Write 100 words.

1. **fairies** : (singular, fairy) small magical creatures with wings.

Before you read

1 **What do you think?**

Who do you think will say the following words from Part Two of the story? Romeo or Juliet?

1 'I cannot wait to see[1] fair[2] Rosaline.'
2 'I have never loved until now.'
3 'I must kiss you.'
4 'Let's change our names. Then we can love.'
5 'A rose can have any name. It always smells sweet.'
6 'Love has sent me here to you.'
7 'Will you be true?'[3]
8 'It is very sad and sweet to say goodnight. But tomorrow we will be married.'

1. **I cannot wait to see** : I am very excited about seeing.
2. **fair** : beautiful.
3. **'will you be true?'** : (here) will you always love me?

2 **Vocabulary**

Here are some words from Part Two. Match them with the pictures.

A a mask   B a dove   C a cheek   D wings   E a crow   F lips

Now read and listen to Part Two and check your ideas for exercise 1.

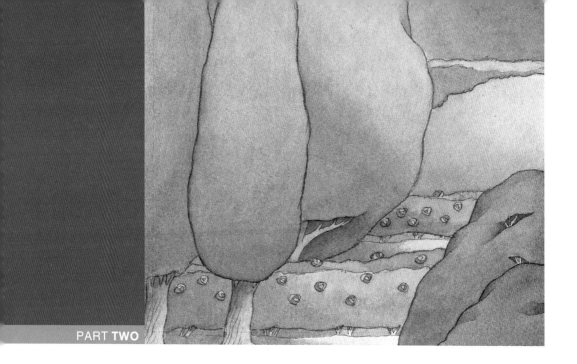

The Garden of the Capulets

omeo went to the party with Benvolio and his friend, Mercutio. They were all wearing masks. It was very dangerous for the Montagues and their friends to go to a party in the house of the Capulets.

'I cannot wait to see [1] fair [2] Rosaline,' said Romeo as they approached [3] the house.

Lord Capulet welcomed them. 'Come in, gentlemen. Dance and drink and eat. Enjoy yourselves.' He did not recognise the son of his enemy, Lord Montague.

He spoke to all the guests. 'Now, girls, dance to the music. When I was younger, I whispered sweet things in the ears of the ladies. But now I am old. My dancing days are finished. I'll sit here with the old people and talk about the past.'

---

1. **I cannot wait to see** : I am very excited about seeing.
2. **fair** : beautiful.
3. **approached** : came near.

As they went into the house, Romeo saw Juliet for the first time. He forgot Rosaline! He fell in love!

'Who is that lady?' asked Romeo. 'She is more beautiful than the moon. She is like a bright jewel [1] in the darkness. She is like a dove among crows. I have never loved until now.'

But Tybalt recognised Romeo's voice. 'It is a Montague. Bring me my sword. It is a great insult for a Montague to come here to laugh at our party. I will kill him.'

'What's the matter, Tybalt?' asked Lord Capulet.

'That man in the mask is a Montague, uncle.'

'Be calm, Tybalt. Is it Romeo? He has a good reputation in Verona. This is a party. I want no trouble [2] in my house. Let him enjoy himself.'

'No, uncle. He is our enemy.'

'Don't be cheeky, [3] young man. I am the master in this house. You must do as I say.'

Tybalt did not agree but he did not want to make Lord Capulet angry. 'I will leave the party. I cannot stay here with a Montague in the room. But I will not forget. Romeo will have a good time tonight but tomorrow he will pay!'

Romeo went to Juliet and talked to her. He did not know who she was. He took her hand gently in his.

'My lips are ready to kiss you,' he said softly. [4]

'I do not know you,' protested Juliet.

'I must kiss you,' insisted Romeo.

1. **jewel** : a diamond, for example.
2. **trouble** : problems.
3. **cheeky** : rude, not polite.
4. **softly** : in a low, quiet voice.

'Here I am,' said Juliet. 'My lips are here.'

Romeo kissed Juliet. He kissed her a second time.

Then the Nurse came to take Juliet to her mother.

'That is Juliet. She is a Capulet,' the Nurse told Romeo.

Romeo was very surprised and upset. [1] He was in love with the daughter of the enemy of his family.

'Quickly, let's go,' said Benvolio. 'It is dangerous here.'

Juliet asked the Nurse, 'Who is that young man?'

'That is Romeo. He is a Montague.'

Juliet was also very surprised and upset. She was in love with the son of the enemy of her family. 'We can never get married,' she thought.

After they left the party, Mercutio and Benvolio looked for Romeo.

'Look! He's there in the shadows. [2] What's he doing?' said Mercutio.

'He's jumping the wall. He's going into the garden of the Capulets.'

Mercutio called out. 'Romeo! Madman! [3] Lover! He's going to look for Rosaline.'

'Quiet! You'll make him angry,' said Benvolio. 'His love is blind.' [4]

Mercutio laughed. 'Good night, Romeo. He's probably sitting under a tree, dreaming about that girl. He's mad.'

Mercutio and Benvolio went home. The night was silent.

In the dark garden, Romeo suddenly saw a light. Juliet was standing on her balcony. 'She's beautiful,' he thought. 'Her eyes are stars. They give light to the night. Her glove [5] touches her cheek — I would like to be her glove!'

Juliet began to speak to the night. She did not know that Romeo was listening.

'Ah, Romeo,' she sighed. [6]

---

1. **upset** : sad, confused.
2. **shadows** : dark places without light.
3. **Madman** : a man whose actions aren't normal.
4. **blind** : not able to see.
5. **glove** : you wear this on your hand.
6. **sighed** [saɪd] : breathed heavily.

'Speak again, angel,' he whispered. [1]

'O Romeo, Romeo! Why is your name Romeo?

Let's change our names. Then we can love.

Forget that you are a Montague.

Or, if you love me, I will not be a Capulet.

Montague and Capulet are only names.

A rose can have any name. It always smells [2] sweet.'

Romeo called out. [3] 'I will change my name for you.'

'Who's there?' asked Juliet. 'Who is listening in the middle of the night?'

'I will not tell you my name because it is your enemy.'

'I know your voice. Are you Romeo? But how did you get over the garden wall?'

'Love gave me wings. No walls can shut out love.'

'If my family find you, they will murder you.'

'The night hides me. I am safe. Love has sent me here to you.'

Romeo and Juliet talked together. Romeo knew Juliet's secret — she loved him. They decided to get married secretly.

'Will you be true?' asked Juliet.

'Yes, my darling,' replied Romeo. 'I promise by the moon.'

'But the moon changes. Will your love change?'

'Never. I will always love you. Do you love me?'

'I told the night that I loved you and you heard me. But I wish I had been silent.' [4]

'Have you changed your mind?' [5]

'No, my love is as deep as the sea. But I must go. The Nurse is calling. Good night, Romeo.'

'Good night, Juliet.'

The Nurse called: 'Juliet! Juliet!'

'I'm coming, Nurse. Good night.'

'Good night.'

'It is very sad and very sweet to say good night. But tomorrow we will be married.'

---

1. **whispered** : said very quietly.
2. **smells** : (here) has a perfume.
3. **called out** : spoke loudly.
4. **I wish I had been silent** : It was better for me not to speak.
5. **changed your mind** : changed your idea.

Go back to the text

PET **1** **Comprehension check**

For each question, mark the correct letter — A, B, C or D.

1   Why were Romeo and his friends wearing masks at the party?
   A ☐ They didn't want people to recognise them.
   B ☐ It was a fashion of those days.
   C ☐ Because everyone had to wear masks.
   D ☐ Because they had ugly faces.

2   What did Lord Capulet want Tybalt to do?
   A ☐ leave the party
   B ☐ enjoy himself at the party
   C ☐ kill Romeo after the party
   D ☐ do nothing

3   After the party, Romeo went to the Capulets' garden
   A ☐ to look for Rosaline.
   B ☐ to be near Juliet.
   C ☐ to sit under a tree and dream.
   D ☐ to meet Juliet.

4   When Romeo saw Juliet on her balcony, she was
   A ☐ thinking aloud about Romeo.
   B ☐ looking for Romeo in the garden.
   C ☐ waiting for Romeo to come to her.
   D ☐ admiring the beautiful night sky.

2 **Discussion**

Work with a partner. Discuss these questions.

1   When he saw Juliet, Romeo fell in love with her immediately. Why did he forget Rosaline so quickly?

2   Juliet is nearly fourteen years old. There are two weeks before her birthday. She told her mother she was too young to get married. Now she can't wait to marry Romeo. What made her change her mind?

3   Many people think that Juliet is a strong character. For example, she says that she loves Romeo before Romeo says that he loves her. What do you think?

4   Mercutio calls Romeo 'mad' and a 'madman'. Can you think of any examples of 'mad love' from stories, songs or films?

'They decided to get married secretly.'

When we want to describe how somebody does something, we use an adverb.
This kind of adverb is called an adverb of manner.
We usually make an adverb of manner by adding *-ly* to the adjective form.
For example: speak *in a soft way* = speak *softly*
They decided to get married secretly.
For adjectives of more than one syllable ending in *-y*, change the *-y* to *-i*.
For example: *happy — happily*
The following adverbs of manner are irregular:

good(adj) — well(adv)   fast(adj) — fast(adv)   hard(adj) — hard(adv)

3 Adverbs
Write the adverbs from of these adjectives. Make any necessary spelling changes.

angry	....	passionate	....
anxious	....	private	....
beautiful	....	sad	....
immediate	....	stupid	....
lazy	....	sweet	....
loud	....	violent	....
lucky	....	warm	....

4 Complete the sentences below with a suitable adverb from exercise 3.

1   Romeo fell in love with Juliet ....
2   The Prince spoke to the people ....
3   Lord Montague asked Benvolio to speak to Romeo ....
4   Lord Capulet welcomed his guests ....
5   The Nurse called Juliet's name ....
6   Juliet smiled ....
7   The servants behaved ....
8   Romeo and Juliet loved each other ....
9   At the party, the musicians played ....
10   Lady Montague asked about Romeo ....

5 Vocabulary – love and marriage

In Shakespeare's play, Juliet says the following words to say goodnight to Romeo:

1	2	3	4	5	6	7		5	8		8	9	10	11
P	A	R	T	I	N	G		I	S		S	U	C	H

P A R T I N G I S S U C H

8	12	13	13	4		8	14	3	3	14	12
S	W	E	E	T		S	O	R	R	O	W

S W E E T S O R R O W

Each number represents a letter of the alphabet.
If you can find the words in the gaps below, you will find out what Juliet said.

0 The answer for number **1** is 'RING'.
Therefore, 3 = R 5 = I 6 = N 7 = G

1 A married woman wears this on her finger: R I N G
    3 5 6 7

2 When people get married there is a: W E D D I N G
    12 13   5 6 7

3 The woman who gets married is the: B R I D E
    3 5   13

4 The man who gets married is the: B R I D E G R O O M
    3 5   13 7 3 14 14

5 They often get married in a: C h u r c h
    10 11 9 3 10 11

6 They are married in church by a: P r i e s t
    1 3 5 13 8 4

7 Everybody hopes the couple will be: h a p p y
    11 2 1 1

8 But sometimes marriages end in: D I V O R C E
    5   14 3 10 13

9 Romeo and Juliet will marry: I M M I D _ _ L Y
    8 13 10 3 13 4

10 Sometimes people have a broken: h e a r t
    11 13 2 3 4

11 Romeo and Juliet were in: L O V E
    14   13

12 They fell in love at first: S I G h t
    8 5   11 4

13 Rosaline was Romeo's first: G I R L F R I E N D
    5 3   3 5 13 6

What do you think Juliet's words mean? Discuss your ideas with a partner.

T: GRADE 5

6 Speaking: special occasions – weddings

Discuss the following questions with a partner. Before you start, think about the words you will need. Make a list. Use a dictionary if necessary.

1 What does a couple have to do before they can get married in your country?

2 What do the bride and bridegroom usually wear?

3 What happens at the wedding?

4 What happens after the wedding?

7 Writing – Dear Diary, ...

A Imagine you are Juliet or Romeo. You have just said goodnight. Finish this entry in your diary. Begin as follows:

I'm in love with a wonderful boy/girl. We only met tonight for the first time, but tomorrow we're going to get married! ....

....

....

....

Write 35-45 words.

B Alternatively, write an entry in Tybalt's diary. Begin as follows:

Tonight I saw Romeo Montague at our party.

Continue by describing Romeo and what you saw him doing. Describe how you felt. Write about what you would like to do. Finish as follows:

I can't sleep because I'm so angry!

Write 35-45 words.

Tonight I saw Romeo Montague at our party. He was wearing a mask and enjoyed himself like he has been invited. But no one invited him. He has just sneaked into the party. I was just thinking about killing him but my father stopped me. It was terribly annoying.

I can't sleep because I'm so angry!

⑧ Listening

There are seven questions in this exercise.

For each question there are three pictures.

As you listen to the recording choose the correct picture and tick (✓) in the box below it. The first one (0) has been done for you.

0 Where is the speaker standing?

A ✓

B

C

1 Where is Lord Capulet standing?

A

B

C

2 Who have just arrived at the party?

A

B

C

3 Who is on the balcony?

A   B   C

4 Which of these is not at the party?

A   B   C

5 Where is Juliet?

A   B   C

6 What is the Nurse looking at?

 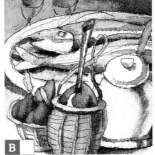 

A   B   C

PET 9 **Writing**

An English friend of yours called Tom likes Shakespeare very much. You want to invite him to a performance of *Romeo and Juliet*.
Write a card or an email to Tom. In the card or email, you should

- invite him to come to the theatre
- tell him the date and time of the performance
- ask him to let you know if he wants to come

Write 35 — 45 words.

PET 10 **Couples**

At the time of *Romeo and Juliet*, women did not generally have the opportunity of a career, so several of Juliet's friends are looking for men to marry.
On the opposite page there are some descriptions of single men in Verona. Decide which man (A-H) would be the most suitable for each woman (1-5). For each of these numbers write the correct letter.

1 ☐ Mariana isn't interested in rich or good-looking men. For her, the most important thing is to have a good family life.
She enjoys cooking and doing housework.

2 ☐ Silvia enjoys going to parties. She thinks it is important to impress her friends who are all very fashionable and sophisticated. She likes wearing expensive jewels and clothes.

3 ☐ Daniela is young and beautiful. She thinks that money is the most important thing in life. She loves gold more than people. She'd like to marry a very rich but young man because she hates the idea of having an old husband.

4 ☐ Francesca is very religious. She spends all her time reading the Bible and praying in church. She is afraid that she will be too busy for this if she is a wife.

5 ☐ Claudia has read a lot of romantic novels. Her idea of a perfect husband is a man who adores his wife. She wants a man who will do everything for her.

Single men from Verona

A Vincenzo has a lot of gold and silver which he keeps in a secret place. He doesn't like spending money. He has decided to get married because he wants a young bride.

B Benedict has a lot of important friends and gets lots of invitations. He is very handsome and wears expensive clothes. He wants an elegant wife who knows how to behave correctly in high society.

C His friends laugh at Dario because he treats women like goddesses. He believes that a man should serve his wife and try to make all her dreams come true. He is young handsome and well-educated.

D Paolo is a merchant who travels a lot so he is often away from home. He has many servants, cooks and gardeners to look after everything in his house. His friends say that his wife will have nothing to do except wait for Paolo to come back from a journey.

E Carlo is not rich or handsome but he is a very kind man. He wants a wife who will stay at home and look after him. He does not want any children as he thinks his wife will pay too much attention to them and not enough to him if she becomes a mother.

F Rodrigo has always wanted to have a lot of children. He isn't rich enough to have a lot of servants so he needs a wife who can help him and look after his house. His female friends think that he is handsome but he says they are all too fond of pleasure to make a good wife for him.

G Inigo is very romantic. He has many girlfriends. He sends roses to them every day and pays musicians to stand under their windows and sing to them. He would probably get bored with a wife very quickly and continue to flirt with the most beautiful women in Verona.

H The only son of one of the richest men in Verona, Stefano is young and handsome but he has no money of his own. However, his father is very ill and the doctors say that he will die soon, so Stefano will inherit all his gold and property.

11 Discussion – falling in love

A 'A man falls in love through his eyes, a woman through her ears.' (Woodrow Wyatt, 1919-1997; British politician and author.)

- Do you think this quotation describes what happens in *Romeo and Juliet*?
- Do you think this quotation describes what happens in real-life love affairs?

B 'love at first sight': a phrase used in English to describe falling in love immediately.

- In groups, make a list of love stories and romantic films that you all know. Do the lovers fall in love "at first sight"? If not, how long does it take them to fall in love: a day, a couple of days, a week, a couple of weeks, ...? Compare the groups' lists in class.
- Do you think that the way that people fall in love in stories and films is similar to what happens in real life?

In Fair[1] Verona

In 2000, UNESCO (the United Nations Educational, Scientific and Cultural Organisation) made Verona a World Heritage Site. This means that UNESCO chose this city of about 270,000 people in the north east of Italy as one of the world's most historically interesting places.

Verona was important during the Roman Empire, and you can still visit buildings from this time. The biggest is the amphitheatre, known as the *Arena*, which was built in the 1st century: 25,000 people could watch shows and gladiators here. It is the third biggest in Italy, after the Colosseum in Rome and the amphitheatre at Capua.

Verona was still important after the end of the Roman Empire, but it became great when the della Scala or Scaligeri family were in power, from 1259 to 1387. Can Grande I (1291–1329) was a patron of the arts: he invited the poet Dante to Verona

'**Juliet's Balcony**' and a statue of Juliet (1969) by Nereo Costantini.

in 1314-15. Interesting and beautiful buildings from the time of the Scaligeri include the castle, known as Castelvecchio (1354-56), and the tombs[2] of the Scaligeri. Their symbol was a ladder, which you can still see in some places.

1. **fair** : beautiful.
2. **tombs** : places, usually above ground, where dead people are put.

The **Roman amphitheatre**. Today you can watch opera here on summer nights.

After the Scaligeri, Verona was under the control of Venice from 1405 to 1797.

In the first lines of his play, Shakespeare says that the story takes place[1] 'in fair Verona', but after the characters never talk about any well-known places in Verona. Some people, however, like to think that Romeo and Juliet lived in Verona, about the time of the Scaligeri.

'Juliet's House' is a 13th-century house in the centre of Verona. The dal Cappello family lived here: cappello in Italian means 'hat', and you can still see a stone hat on the entrance arch.[2] The family name is similar to Cappelletti (how Italians say 'Capulets') and this is why people thought that Shakespeare's Juliet lived here. The city of Verona bought the house in 1905, and there is now a small museum inside. The balcony was added when the house was restored[3] in 1935-40, but many of the thousands of tourists who come here think Juliet stood on it!

1. **takes place** : happens

2. **arch** :

3. **restored** : repaired and cleaned to make it look in a good condition again.

Very near 'Juliet's House' there is a medieval house known as 'Romeo's House'. The Montecchi family (how Italians say 'Montagues') lived in this area, but we can't say that this was their house.

About ten minutes' walk away, near the river, you can visit 'Juliet's Tomb' in the old monastery [1] of San Francesco. Here, in a room underground, there is a large tomb: there are lots of tourists, but no historical connection to the story! But in the old buildings of the monastery (not used any more as a monastery) the city of Verona allows both Italians and foreigners to get married.

'Juliet's Tomb'.

1. **monastery** : building(s) where members of a religious community live.

The **River Adige** in Verona. The bridge is Roman.

1 Comprehension check

1 What buildings in Verona are connected to Romeo and Juliet? Are these connections real or not?

2 The text mentions two historical periods and buildings from these periods. What are the periods and what are the buildings?

2 Discussion

1 What *one* thing did you find most interesting in the text? Compare your choices in class.

2 You are going to Verona for a day of sightseeing (visiting the 'sights', the interesting places). List 5 sights you want to see in your order of preference (1=most interesting for you, 5=least interesting for you). Compare your choices in class.

 INTERNET PROJECT

Connect to the Internet and go to www.blackcat-cideb.com or www.cideb.it . Insert the title or part of the title of the book into our search engine. Open the page for Romeo and Juliet. Click on the Internet project link. Go down the page until you find the title of this book and click on the relevant link for this project.

▶ How many UNESCO World Heritage Sites are there so far?

▶ How many sites are there in your country? How many have you been to?

▶ Choose one other country, and choose the site in it you would most like to visit.

Before you read

1 What happens next

Here are some events from Part Three of the story. Think about the answers to the questions, or discuss them with a partner.

1 Romeo asks his friend Friar Laurence to help him. Why?

2 Tybalt wants to fight Romeo? Why?

3 Juliet meets Romeo at Friar Laurence's cell. Why?

4 Tybalt tells Benvolio and Mercutio that they are his enemies. Why?

5 Romeo doesn't want to fight Tybalt? Why not?

Now read and listen to Part Three and check your ideas.

The Prince of Cats¹

omeo went to see Friar ² Laurence, his friend and teacher. The sun was rising ³ and it was a beautiful morning. The Friar was working in his garden. He was an expert gardener who knew all the plants — the poisonous ⁴ ones, the medicinal ⁵ ones, the good ones and the bad ones.

'Friar,' said Romeo, 'I want to get married.'

'To Rosaline?' asked the Friar.

'No, I have forgotten Rosaline. She is nothing to me. I love Juliet and she loves me. You must help us. We want to get married today.'

'What? I see that young men's love is not in their hearts but in their eyes!'

'But Friar, you often told me that I was foolish to love Rosaline. Juliet is my true love.'

1. **Prince of Cats** : Tybalt is dangerous, like a cat. 'Tybalt' was also a name given to cats in medieval stories.
2. **Friar** : member of a Catholic Christian community.
3. **rising** : coming up (*rise-rose-risen*).
4. **poisonous** (plants) : (plants that) will kill you if you eat them.
5. **medicinal** (plants) : (plants that) will make you better if you are ill.

'Well, perhaps your marriage will make the Capulets and the Montagues friends. It's a good thing for Verona. I'll help you.'

Benvolio and Mercutio were looking for Romeo in the streets of Verona.

'Poor Romeo,' said Benvolio. 'His heart is broken. Rosaline does not love him.'

'That's not his only problem,' replied Mercutio. 'Tybalt has challenged [1] him. He has sent a letter to his house. He wants to fight him.'

'But Tybalt is dangerous.'

'Yes. Tybalt is the Prince of Cats. He's an artist with his sword. [2] Romeo is a lamb. [3] He will die.'

'Here comes Romeo.'

'He's already dead. Rosaline has killed him with her cold eye! To him, she is more beautiful than Cleopatra. [4] She is the most beautiful woman that ever lived. Lovers are fools!'

Mercutio called to Romeo. 'Where did you go last night after the party? You ran away from us.'

'I'm sorry. I was busy.'

'Busy with Rosaline, eh? Forget love, Romeo. Remember your friends. Friendship is more important than love.'

'But look!' said Mercutio. 'Here comes a fat old woman.'

It was the Nurse. Juliet had sent her to find Romeo. 'I must speak alone with you, sir,' she said.

Mercutio laughed. 'Is this your new girlfriend?' he asked.

1. **challenged him** : invited Romeo to fight.
2. **an artist with his sword** : he uses his sword very well.
3. **a lamb** : a young sheep; (here) not a violent person.
4. **Cleopatra** : a queen of Egypt (69-30 BC) who fell in love with the Roman general Mark Antony. Shakespeare wrote a play about their love affair.

'Go away,' said Romeo. 'Now, Nurse, what do you want?'

'First of all, I want you to promise that you will be kind to Juliet. She's very young. You must not hurt her.'

'I love her.'

'Then what do you want me to tell her?'

'Tell Juliet to come to Friar Laurence's cell [1] this afternoon. We will get married there.'

'I love Juliet, sir. I remember when she was a little child. Look after her when you are her husband.'

The Nurse went back to Juliet, who was waiting anxiously. She told her the news. 'Tell your parents that you are going to pray,' [2] said the Nurse. 'Then go to see Friar Laurence.'

The two lovers got ready [3] for their secret wedding.

In the afternoon the sun was shining. Romeo went secretly to Friar Laurence's cell.

'The day is bright,' said the Friar. 'It's a sign that the future will be happy.'

'I don't care [4] if I die tomorrow. It's enough that Juliet is mine.'

'Don't be so passionate. It's better to love moderately. Then love will last [5] longer.'

At last Juliet arrived. She was very nervous. So was Romeo. They were very young but very much in love. Friar Laurence was like a father to them. He took them into his cell and they were married.

Meanwhile, Benvolio and Mercutio were walking in the streets of Verona. 'Let's go home,' said Benvolio. 'The Capulets are out in the streets. If we meet them, we will have to fight. In this hot weather young men do mad things.'

---

1. **cell** : small room in which a friar lives.
2. **pray** : speak to God.
3. **got ready** : prepared themselves.
4. **I don't care** : it is not important to me.
5. **last** : continue.

Romeo and Juliet

'Don't worry. We're safe.'

'Here come the Capulets. Tybalt is there!'

'The Prince of Cats. I am not afraid.'

Tybalt approached Mercutio. 'I want to speak with you.'

'Do you want to speak or to fight?'

'You are not a Montague but a friend of Romeo. That makes you my enemy.'

'Be careful,' said Benvolio. 'We're in the public streets. If you fight, the Prince will be angry.'

At that moment, Romeo came back from his secret wedding.

'Fight, you villain!' [1] shouted Tybalt.

Romeo did not want to fight because Tybalt was Juliet's cousin. 'I am not a villain. And I will not fight with you.'

Mercutio was angry because he thought that Romeo was a coward. [2] He took out his own sword.

1. **villain** : bad person.
2. **coward** : someone who is afraid.

'What do you want?' asked Tybalt.

'I want one of your nine lives, Prince of Cats!'

'I will fight you as Romeo is too afraid to fight,' said Tybalt.

Romeo came between Mercutio and Tybalt as they began to fight. 'Stop fighting. The Prince will be angry. He will punish you. Stop fighting! Stop, Tybalt! Stop, good Mercutio!' shouted Romeo.

But Tybalt took the opportunity to kill Mercutio. His sword passed under Romeo's arm as he stood between them. Then Tybalt ran quickly away.

Mercutio groaned. [1] 'Aagh! I am hurt. I am dying. Romeo, this quarrel [2] between your families has killed me.'

'Are you badly hurt?' asked Romeo.

'A scratch, [3] a scratch. It's enough. Bring me a doctor.'

'Be brave, Mercutio. It cannot be so bad.'

'Look for me tomorrow in my grave. [4] The Prince of Cats has killed me. Why did you come between us?'

'I wanted to help...'

Mercutio fell to the ground and died. It was Romeo's fault. [5] His friend was dead.

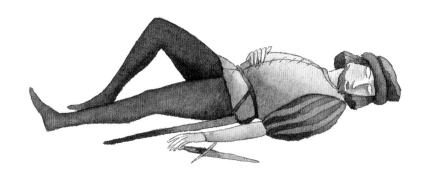

1. **groaned** : cried with pain.
2. **quarrel** : argument, fight.
3. **scratch** : a small cut; for example, a cat can scratch you.
4. **grave** : the place for a dead person under the ground.
5. **It was Romeo's fault** : Romeo caused the bad thing to happen.

Go back to the text

1 **Comprehension check**
Answer the questions.

1 Why did Friar Laurence agree to help Romeo?
2 Why was Tybalt a dangerous man?
3 Where did Romeo want Juliet to meet him that afternoon?
4 How did the two lovers feel when they met?
5 Who wanted to fight Tybalt?
6 What was the result of the fight?

2 **Discussion**
Work with a partner. Explain what the following extracts from Part Three mean.

1 (Friar Laurence) 'What? I see that young men's love is not in their hearts but in their eyes!'
2 (Mercutio) 'He is already dead. Rosaline has killed him with her cold eye! To him, she is more beautiful than Cleopatra. She is the most beautiful woman that ever lived. Lovers are fools!'

3 **Vocabulary – animals and character**
We often associate animals with certain characteristics. In Part Three, Mercutio calls Tybalt 'the Prince of Cats', meaning that he is dangerous. He calls Romeo a 'lamb', meaning that he is gentle and innocent. Which of the animals in the pictures (1-9) are usually associated with the adjectives in (A-I)? Use a dictionary if necessary.

1 ▢   2 ▢   3 ▢

4 ▢   5 ▢   6 ▢

A stupid	**B** cunning	**C** graceful	**D** wise	**E** blind
F proud	**G** quiet	**H** brave	**I** greedy	

4 **Adjectives**

Think of an adjective that you associate with these animals.

Work in small groups. Compare your ideas.

'The Prince of Cats has killed me.'

Look at these sentences from Part Three.

*Tybalt **has challenged** him. He **has sent** a letter to his house.*
*The Prince of Cats **has killed** me.*

The verbs are in the Present Perfect Simple tense. We use this tense when we are talking about an action that happened at an undefined time in the past but has results in the present. It is often a recent action.

The adverbs *yet* (in questions and negative statements), *already* (in positive statements) and *just* (in positive statements and questions) are common with this use.

***Has** Romeo **received** Tybalt's letter **yet**?*
*The Capulets **have already had** their party.*
*Tybalt **has just killed** Mercutio.*

53

5 The Present Perfect Simple

Complete these sentences about some of the characters in the story. Use the Present Perfect Simple.

0 Romeo/already/forget/Rosaline
   Romeo has already forgotten Rosaline.
1 Friar Laurence/just/finish/watering his plants.
2 Juliet/tell/her parents about her marriage yet?
3 Mercutio's friends/already/take/his body to his house.
4 Tybalt/not hear/the news about Mercutio's death yet.
5 The Capulets/already/choose/Paris as a husband for their daughter.
6 The Montagues/make peace with the Capulets yet?
7 The Nurse/just/prepare/Juliet's bath.
8 Romeo and Juliet/spend/a night together yet?

6 Are these statements true for you? Write Yes or No.

		Yes	No
1	I've just had lunch.	☐	☐
2	I haven't thought about my future yet.	☐	☐
3	I've already met the girl/boy that I want to marry.	☐	☐
4	I've just had my fifteenth birthday.	☐	☐
5	I haven't passed my driving test yet.	☐	☐
6	I've already read the end of this story.	☐	☐

Now work with a partner. Ask and answer like this:

Have you just had lunch? Yes, I have./No, I haven't.

7 Listening – questions

You will hear a conversation between Juliet and the Nurse. The Nurse has returned from the town, where she has seen Romeo. Juliet wants to know the news but the Nurse makes her wait. Listen carefully. Complete Juliet's questions.

Juliet: Where (1) .... ?
         Why (2) .... ? Ah, she's here.
         Have (3) .... ?
Nurse: I am very tired. I have run from the town. My bones [1] ache. [2]
Juliet: What (4) .... ?
Nurse: Well, I have seen Romeo. He is handsome, young and polite. But have you had dinner yet?

1. **bones** : parts of the skeleton.   2. **ache** : hurt, cause pain.

54

Juliet: Nurse, don't ask stupid questions.
What (**5**) .... ?

Nurse: My head aches. I am very tired.

Juliet: I am sorry for you.
But sweet Nurse, what (**6**) .... ?

Nurse: He says... Where is your mother?

Juliet: She's in the house. But please be quick.
Is (**7**) .... ?

Nurse: Don't be angry. I have run all over the city for you. Next time, go and ask Romeo yourself.

Juliet: Sweet Nurse, please tell me.
Did (**8**) .... ?

Nurse: He wants to marry you at Friar Laurence's cell this afternoon.

Juliet: Aaah! Thank you, Nurse.

8 **The story so far**

Look at the pictures on the next two pages. They tell the story of Parts One, Two and Three of *Romeo and Juliet*.

1 start a fight   2 tell   3 decide

4 go   5 see   6 kiss

55

7 jump 8 talk 9 meet

10 get married 11 fight 12 die

What are the Past Simple forms of the verbs below the pictures?

1	start	....	7	jump	....
2	tell	....	8	talk	....
3	decide	....	9	meet	....
4	go	....	10	get	....
5	see	....	11	fight	....
6	kiss	....	12	die	....

9 **Writing**

Write a summary of the story so far. Use the verbs above and include the following words and expressions:

one day   then   later   at the party   after the party
the next day   in the afternoon

Begin like this:

The Montagues and the Capulets hated each other.
One day Tybalt, a Capulet, started a fight with Benvolio, a Montague, in the streets.
Then the Prince of Verona ...

PET ⑩ Feuds

Read the text below and choose the correct word for each space.
For each question, mark the letter next to the correct word — A, B, C or D.

A feud is an angry disagreement (0) ..B.. two people or two groups of people that continues (1) .... a long time, sometimes (2) .... hundreds of years. The two sides do not fight or argue all the time, but the fighting can start at (3) .... time, even for a very small (4) .... There are many causes of feuds in history, (5) .... as murder, insult, economic competition, and so on. Shakespeare never (6) .... us why the feud in Verona exists, and the characters never give a reason (7) .... the two families hate each (8) .... Shakespeare is interested (9) .... drama rather than history. In modern (10) .... of the play the lovers sometimes come from different social classes or ethnic backgrounds.

0	A among	B between	C around	D of
1	A since	B for	C ago	D from
2	A also	B much	C so	D even
3	A some	B any	C a	D certain
4	A reason	B cause	C motive	D start
5	A like	B for	C examples	D such
6	A says	B explains	C tells	D reveals
7	A why	B for	C that	D because
8	A ones	B other	C one	D others
9	A for	B about	C by	D in
10	A shows	B varieties	C versions	D kinds

(0 B between is circled)

⑪ Discussion

Can you think of other reasons for a feud which were not mentioned above? Could they be used in a modern version of *Romeo and Juliet*?

Before you read

① Characters

Here are some sentences about Part Four. Complete them with the name of a character in the story. Then read and listen to Part Four and check your ideas.

1 Romeo kills ....
2 .... says that Romeo can't live in Verona any more.
3 Romeo goes to hide [1] with ....
4 .... takes a message from Juliet to Romeo
5 Lord Capulet tells .... that he can marry Juliet on Thursday.

1. **hide:** (*hide-hid-hidden*) stay in a secret place.

Fortune's Fool [1]

t that moment Tybalt returned.

'Boy!' shouted Tybalt. 'You came here with Mercutio and you will die as he did!'

Romeo was so angry that he lost control. He took out his sword and fought with Tybalt. He killed him.

'He killed my friend. Now he is dead. He is with Mercutio. Juliet, your love made me a coward but now I am brave.'

Benvolio took his arm. 'Romeo, you must escape. The people are coming. The Prince will punish you with death.' [2]

'Oh, I am Fortune's fool!' With those words, Romeo ran away.

Soon the citizens arrived, followed by the Prince. They saw Mercutio and Tybalt lying dead on the ground.

'Where are the people who began this fight?' asked the Prince angrily.

'I can tell you the complete story,' promised Benvolio.

---

1. **Fortune's Fool** : a person who has very bad luck.
2. **punish you with death** : Benvolio thinks the Prince will kill Romeo because he has killed Tybalt.

Romeo and Juliet

'Oh Tybalt!' screamed [1] Lady Capulet. 'My brother's child. He has been murdered. A Montague must die for this.'

'Romeo wanted to stop the fight,' explained Benvolio. 'But Tybalt killed Mercutio. Then Romeo killed Tybalt.'

'He's lying!' [2] said Lady Capulet. 'He's a Montague. Romeo killed Tybalt. So Romeo must not live.'

'Romeo killed Tybalt. But Tybalt killed Mercutio,' said the Prince.

'Mercutio was Romeo's friend,' agreed Lord Montague. 'Romeo was right to kill his friend's killer.'

The Prince spoke seriously. 'No! It is wrong to kill. We banish [3] Romeo from Verona! If I find him in the city, he will die! We must not show mercy [4] to murderers.'

Those were the Prince's final words. Romeo had to leave Verona and never return.

Juliet was waiting for Romeo, her new husband. She wanted the night to come quickly so that they could be together. But when the Nurse arrived, she brought bad news.

'He is dead!'

'Who is dead?'

'I saw the body with my own eyes. He is dead.'

'What? Is Romeo dead?'

'No, Tybalt is dead. Romeo has killed him. Romeo is banished, he must leave Verona.'

'Did Romeo kill my cousin? He's a villain. But I love him.'

---

1. **screamed** : shouted in a high voice.
2. **lying** : not telling the truth.
3. **banish** : send away from the city forever.
4. **mercy** : pity, forgiveness.

Juliet was very unhappy. 'Your father and mother are crying for Tybalt,' the Nurse told her.

'I will cry for him too,' said Juliet. 'But I will cry longer for Romeo. I will never see him again. I will kill myself.'

'No,' said the Nurse. 'Romeo is hiding with Friar Laurence. I will bring him to you.'

'Yes, Nurse, bring him to me quickly. Give him this ring. He must come and say his last goodbye.'

Romeo was talking to Friar Laurence. 'Everything is finished. I must leave Verona and never see Juliet again. Even a cat or a dog or a mouse may look at Juliet. But I cannot. Give me poison or a knife to kill myself.'

'You are mad. The Prince has shown mercy. He lets you live.'

'You are old, Friar. But I am young and in love. I want to die.'

'No, be brave. You must go to Mantua. You will be safe there. I will send you news about Juliet. One day you will be together again. But here is the Nurse.'

'How is Juliet?' Romeo asked her immediately.

'She cries and cries. First she calls out Tybalt's name, then she calls for Romeo. Then she falls on her bed.'

'Tonight, go with the Nurse,' said the Friar. 'See Juliet for the last time.'

Romeo went back to the house of the Capulets. The Nurse took him into the garden. Nobody saw them.

'Here is a ladder,'[1] she said. 'Climb up and go through the window.'

So Romeo spent his wedding night with Juliet.

---

1. **ladder** :

Romeo and Juliet

Downstairs, in the house of the Capulets, Lord and Lady Capulet were talking. Lord Paris was with them.

'I will talk to Juliet. She will marry you next Wednesday...'

'That's too soon,' said Lady Capulet.

'On Thursday then. Tybalt is dead. There must be something good for the Capulet family — Juliet's wedding! I am her father. She will do as I say.'

Paris was very happy because he loved Juliet. Lord Capulet told his wife to see Juliet in the morning. She must prepare for her marriage. Her parents did not know that Juliet was already married to Romeo, the killer of her cousin Tybalt.

'I wish it was Thursday tomorrow,' said Paris.

'Well, goodbye until then,' said Lord Capulet. 'On Thursday, my daughter will marry you. I promise.'

In the morning, Romeo left Juliet. He had to escape to Mantua before the Prince found him.

'Must you go?' asked Juliet. 'It's still night. The nightingale[1] is singing, not the lark.'[2]

'Look at the sky. The sun is rising. But I want to stay.'

'Go. It is dangerous for you here. But I want you to stay. Goodbye, sweet Romeo. Will I ever see you again?'

'Goodbye. I will think of you every second of the day.'

They kissed. Then Romeo climbed down the ladder.

'I can see only bad luck in the future,' said Juliet. 'I seem to see you dead.'

'Our sadness makes us think in this way. I will write every day. Goodbye.'

'Please, God, send him back to me again.'

---

1. **the nightingale** : a night bird.   2. **the lark** : a morning bird.

Go back to the text

1 Comprehension check
Answer the questions.

1 Did Romeo do the right thing when he killed Tybalt?
2 What did the Prince decide?
3 Did Juliet hate Romeo for killing Tybalt?
4 Where did Friar Laurence tell Romeo to go?
5 What didn't Lord and Lady Capulet know?
6 What could Juliet see in the future for her and Romeo?

2 Discussion
Work with a partner. Discuss these questions.

1 Was Romeo right to kill Tybalt?
2 What should Juliet do now?

3 Vocabulary – good luck and bad luck
Look at these words:

lucky   luckier   luckiest   luckily   unluckily

unlucky   unluckier   unluckiest   luck

All these words come from the word 'luck'. Write one suitable word from the list in each gap in the sentences below. You can use the same word more than once.

1 Romeo and Juliet are the .... lovers in history.
2 Mercutio had very bad ....
3 ...., the Prince did not find Romeo.
4 If Romeo has good ...., he will see Juliet again.
5 Romeo is not very ....
6 It was .... that Romeo and Juliet came from families which were enemies.
7 During their fight, Tybalt was .... than Mercutio.
8 ...., Tybalt recognised Romeo at the party.
9 Before he left, Benvolio said, 'Good ....' to Romeo.
10 'I will be the .... man in the world if you marry me,' said Romeo.

63

4 Vocabulary – word formation

A How many words can you make from these words? Use a dictionary to help you find some adjectives, adverbs, nouns and verbs, as well as some positive and negative forms.

fortune   succeed   fail   die   friend   love   marry

B Now write a couple of sentences using some of the words you have found. Try to include more than one word in each sentence. For example:

Some people think that friendship can be more important than love and marriage, but I don't agree with them.

'Juliet was waiting for Romeo, her new husband.'

Past Simple and Past Continuous

Downstairs in the house of the Capulets, Lord and Lady Capulet **were talking**.

The verb is in the Past Continuous tense. We use this tense for
- an action in the past that has a duration
- an action that was interrupted by another action expressed by the Past Simple
- describing a background scene when we tell a story

5 Past Continuous

Put the verbs in brackets in the Past Continuous (*was/were -ing*) or Past Simple form. Remember that some verbs have an irregular past form (e.g. *see - saw*)

1 It (*be*) a terrible day! Everyone (*fight*) in the streets of Verona.
2 The Prince (*want*) peace in his city.
3 Romeo (*walk*) alone in the fields when Benvolio (*meet*) him.
4 Juliet (*think*) about Romeo when her mother (*come*) into the room.
5 While Romeo and Juliet (*kiss*), the Nurse (*see*) them.
6 Everybody at the party (*wear*) a mask but Tybalt (*recognise*) Romeo's voice.
7 While Romeo (*stand*) under her balcony, Juliet (*begin*) to speak.
8 It (*be*) a beautiful morning and Friar Laurence (*work*) in his garden.
9 While the Nurse (*talk*) to Romeo, Juliet (*wait*) anxiously at home.
10 Tybalt (*kill*) Mercutio while Romeo (*try*) to stop them fighting.

6 Listening – horoscopes

PET

You will hear someone talking about horoscopes. For each question, put a tick (✓) in the correct box.

1 Capricorns will

A ☐ be very successful in love.
B ☐ fall in love.
C ☐ travel to interesting places in this country.

2   Cancers will have

A ☐   a similar social life to Capricorns.

B ☐   a worse social life than Capricorns.

C ☐   a much better social life than Capricorns.

3   For Leos, it will be a
    good year for

A ☐   love and social life.

B ☐   work and travel.

C ☐   love and health.

4   There will be broken
    hearts

A ☐   for Librans born after the new moon.

B ☐   for all Librans.

C ☐   for some Librans.

5   In general, Librans may
    well have

A ☐   a bad year.

B ☐   a good year.

C ☐   a bad first half of the year.

6   The horoscopes include
    predictions about

A ☐   marriage, social life and travel.

B ☐   work, love and money.

C ☐   work, love and social life.

7 Discussion

Here is how we say the star signs in English:

Aries (the Ram)   Taurus (the Bull)   Gemini (the Twins)   Cancer (the Crab)

Leo (the Lion)   Virgo (the Virgin)   Libra (the Balance)   Scorpio (the Scorpion)

Sagittarius (the Archer)   Capricorn (the Goat)   Aquarius (the Water Carrier)

Pisces (the Fish)

A   Find out from books or the Internet what the qualities of the star signs are.

B   Decide what would be suitable star signs for Romeo and Juliet.

C   What would be suitable star signs for Tybalt, Mercutio or Benvolio?

PET 8 Writing

Your English teacher has asked you to write a story.
Your story must begin with this sentence:

It was the unluckiest day of Kevin Brown's life.

Write your story in about 100 words.

Settings[1] and Sources[2]

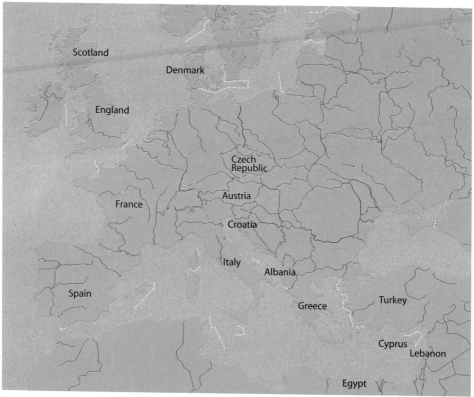

Look at the list of all of Shakespeare's plays on the next page. They are in the order that we think he wrote them. There are 36 of them (number 1 on the list includes 3 plays, and number 13 includes 2 plays).

Don't worry if you don't understand all the names of his plays in the left-hand column. Read the settings in the right-hand column.

1 How many of the settings are in England?

2 How many of the settings are not in England? Can you find these places on the map above?

When you have answered these questions, turn to page 68.

---

1. **setting** : the place where a play, story, film etc. takes place. (Setting can also include the historical period.) You can also say a story is 'set' somewhere.
2. **sources** : (here) books or people where you go to get information or ideas.

1	Henry VI (3 plays: parts 1, 2 & 3)	England.
2	The Comedy of Errors	Syracuse & Ephesus (Turkey).
3	Titus Andronicus	Rome.
4	Richard III	England.
5	The Taming of the Shrew	Verona & Padua.
6	The Two Gentlemen of Verona	Verona & Milan.
7	A Midsummer Night's Dream	Athens.
8	Love's Labour's Lost	Navarre (this old region is now northern Spain & southern France).
9	Romeo and Juliet	Verona.
10	Richard II	England.
11	The Merchant of Venice	Venice.
12	King John	England.
13	Henry IV (2 plays: parts 1 & 2)	England.
14	The Merry Wives of Windsor	England.
15	Much Ado About Nothing	Messina.
16	Henry V	England & France.
17	Julius Caesar	Rome.
18	As You Like It	An imaginary country (a mix of England & France).
19	Twelfth Night	Illyria (this old region is now Croatia, Montenegro & Albania).
20	Hamlet	Elsinore, Denmark.
21	All's Well That Ends Well	Roussillon (a region in France near the Pyrenees & Mediterranean) & Florence.
22	Troilus and Cressida	Troy (Turkey).
23	Measure for Measure	Vienna.
24	Othello	Venice & Cyprus.
25	King Lear	England.
26	Macbeth	Scotland.
27	Antony and Cleopatra	Rome & Egypt.
28	Coriolanus	Rome.
29	Timon of Athens	Athens.
30	Pericles	Tyre (Lebanon), Tarsus & Ephesus (Turkey), Mytilene (on Lesbos, a Greek island).
31	Cymbeline	England.
32	The Winter's Tale	Sicily & Bohemia (a mix of the Czech Republic & an imaginary country).
33	The Tempest	An unnamed southern Mediterranean island.

The setting of the plays about English history is, of course, England (numbers 1, 4, 10, 12, 13 & 16 in the list). Four other plays have English settings (14, 18, 25 & 31), and *Macbeth* is set in Scotland: so, fourteen plays are set in Britain. But twelve are set in Italy! Why is this?

Like all writers of his time, Shakespeare took other people's stories and changed them. Only three of his plays are original. He often used Italian stories, which is why so many of his plays are set in Italy.

For his English history plays, Shakespeare read the historian Holinshed. For his Roman plays, such as *Julius Caesar*, he read the Greek historian Plutarch in an

English translation. Sometimes he took a play by another playwright that was a success in London ten years before and rewrote it: he did this with his two most famous plays, *King Lear* and *Hamlet*. But many of his sources are Italian stories by writers such as Boccaccio, Ariosto and Cinthio, which he read in English or French translations.

Where does *Romeo and Juliet* come from? The story started in folklore, and it was first written down by the Italian Masuccio Salernitano in 1476. The setting is the Italian city of Siena in the 15th century, and the lovers are called Mariotto and Giannozza.

The Italian writer **Giovanni Boccaccio** (1313-75). Shakespeare and other English writers used his collection of stories **The Decameron** as sources.

DOMINVS IOHANNES BOCCACCIVS

Then Luigi da Porto (1485-1529) from Vicenza (a town only 50 kilometres from Verona) wrote a new version of the story, which was published in 1530. In his *Giulietta e Romeo* or *Historia novellamente ritrovata di due nobili amanti* ("a retold story of two noble lovers") he changed the setting to Verona at the time of Bartolomeo della Scala (1299-1304), one of the Scaligeri lords of Verona (see page 42). This is why so many people think – wrongly – that the story is based on real historical events. Da Porto also invented the feuding families (calling them Capuleti and Montecchi) and changed the lovers' names to Romeo and Giulietta. But da Porto's Giulietta is eighteen, and the lovers meet at her balcony several times.

In 1554, the Italian Matteo Bandello wrote a version with small changes. This was translated into French in 1559 by Pierre Boaistuau, and this version was translated several times into English.

Boaistuau's French names for the families – Capulet and Montague – are used in English versions. Arthur Brooke's 1562 poem, *The Tragicall Historye of Romeus and Juliet*, was very popular, and Shakespeare used this version as his source. But Shakespeare made important changes. Brooke's story lasts nine months; Shakespeare reduced this to three or four days. Brooke reduced Juliet's age to sixteen, but Shakespeare reduced this even more: his Juliet will be fourteen in two weeks' time.

For Brooke, the lovers are wrong. He writes that they follow 'unhonest desire' and do not follow the 'authority and advice of parents and friends'. His message is that it is wrong to disobey parents. [1] But in Shakespeare's play the lovers become heroes: Juliet in particular is very brave when she disobeys her parents.

Settings in films

There are more than 350 films of Shakespeare's plays and hundreds of television versions. Films often change Shakespeare's settings. Here are just three recent examples: *Richard III* (1996), with Sir Ian McKellen, set in London in the 1930s: *Romeo + Juliet* (1997) set in modern California (more on pages 94-6): *Hamlet* (2000), with Ethan Hawke, set in modern New York in the world of big business.

---

1. **disobey parents** : not do what parents say must be done.

Many films use the stories from Shakespeare's plays, but not Shakespeare's words. In his last play, *The Tempest*, Prospero the magician lives on a island with a supernatural spirit called Ariel. In the cult American science fiction film *Forbidden Planet* (1956), the island is a planet far away in space, the magician is a scientist and the spirit is a robot! The Japanese film director Akira Kurosawa (1910-98) made two great Shakespearean films set in Japan in the middle ages, where the characters are Samurai fighters: *Throne of Blood* (1957) uses the story of *Macbeth* and *Ran* (1985) uses the story of *King Lear*. Shakespeare took other people's stories and changed them, and film directors continue to do this.

Doctor Morbius (Prospero) and Robby the robot (Ariel). **Forbidden Planet**, like all science fiction, reveals more about when it was made (the 1950s) than about the future!

A poster for **Throne of Blood**. Kurosawa made many Samurai films. His *Seven Samurai* (1954) was remade by Hollywood as a Western, *The Magnificent Seven* (1960).

1 Comprehension check

1 How many of Shakespeare's plays have Italian settings? Why is this?

2 How many versions of the Romeo and Juliet story were there before Shakespeare wrote his play?

3 How did Shakespeare change Arthur Brooke's story?

2 Discussion

1 What do you think is the most interesting change that Shakespeare made to Brooke's story?

2 In the Romantic Age in Europe (first half of the 19th century) people started to think that it was important to be original. But in Shakespeare's times, the greatest writer was the one who could tell old stories best. Is it important for you that a story or film is completely original?

3 There have been many versions of the Romeo and Juliet story. Do you know any other stories that have been told many times, in different versions?

4 Choose a very famous story from your culture. Invent another setting for a new film of it. Think about time (a different historical place, or even the future) and place. You can change or omit details, but the audience should be able to realise what story the film is based on.

3 Writing

Choose a famous story either from your culture or from anywhere in the world. Write a short summary of it (150-200 words) in a changed setting. Will the reader of your summary recognise the original story?

Before you read

1 Listening

Listen to Part Five of the story. Are the statements true or false? Put a tick in the appropriate box.

	T	F
1 Lady Capulet tells Juliet to stop crying.	☐	☐
2 Lord Capulet is kind to Juliet.	☐	☐
3 The Nurse tells Juliet to go and see Friar Laurence.	☐	☐
4 Juliet agrees to marry Paris.	☐	☐
5 Juliet's body is taken to the church.	☐	☐

Now read and listen to Part Five and check your ideas.

My Lady's Dead!

arly next morning, Lady Capulet visited Juliet in her
bedroom. 'Daughter, are you awake?'

'It's very early. I am not well,' answered Juliet.

'Are you still crying for your cousin Tybalt? It's good to
cry. But now it's time to stop.'

'Let me cry more for my poor cousin.'

'Well, really you should cry because Romeo, his killer, is still alive.'

'Yes, mother. I wish I could see Romeo now and... kill him.'

'I will send a servant to Mantua to poison him,' promised Lady Capulet.
'He will not live long. But Juliet, I have good news for you. You will get
married to Paris early next Thursday morning. Then you will be happy.'

'No, mother. It's impossible. I don't want to get married so soon. Tell my
father this. As you know, I hate Romeo. He has killed my cousin. But I'd
rather[1] marry Romeo than Paris.'

'Here comes your father. Tell him yourself.'

---

1. **I'd rather** : I would prefer to.

'What?' said Lord Capulet. 'Are you still crying? Wife, have you told her the news?'

'Yes. The little fool thanks you but she won't marry Paris.'

Lord Capulet was very angry. 'Lord Paris is a very fine gentleman. This is a great opportunity.'

'Thank you, father, but I will not marry him.'

'Are you too proud [1] to marry him? Put on a wedding dress next Thursday and go with Paris to the church. If you don't, I'll pull you there by the hair.'

'Good father, listen to me.'

'Don't argue [2] with me. Go to the church next Thursday. I'm glad we have no more children like this.'

'Please don't be angry with my little Juliet, sir,' said the Nurse.

'Shut up, you fat old fool!'

'Be calm,' Lady Capulet told him.

'I have decided. If you don't obey me, [3] I will throw you out in the street.'

When her parents had gone, Juliet asked the Nurse for advice. [4]

'I already have a husband that I love. What should I do?'

'Well, Romeo is not here. Paris is a fine gentleman, it's true. He is more handsome than Romeo. Forget Romeo and marry Paris.'

'Do you speak from your heart?'

'Of course,' said the Nurse.

Juliet realised that she couldn't trust [5] the Nurse. She went to Friar Laurence to ask his advice.

---

1. **are you too proud** : (here) do you think you are too superior?
2. **argue** : disagree.
3. **obey me** : follow my instructions, do as I say.
4. **advice** : a suggestion about the best thing to do.
5. **trust** : believe in.

The Friar was very worried. Paris was talking to him and had told him that he would marry Juliet.

'Does she love you?' asked the Friar.

'I don't know. We haven't talked about love because she's weeping [1] for her cousin's death. But our marriage will make her happy again.'

'But look, here comes Juliet.'

'Welcome, my lady and my wife,' said Paris. 'Have you come to tell the Friar that you love me?'

'I cannot answer that,' said Juliet. 'But please, let me talk to the Friar privately.'

When they were alone, the Friar told Juliet to be happy. 'If you are brave enough, I have a plan that will help you and Romeo. You will be together again.'

'What must I do? I will do anything for Romeo, my husband.'

'Go home and agree to marry Paris.'

'No! I cannot.'

'Listen carefully. On Wednesday night, go to your bedroom alone. Take this bottle and drink the liquid. It's a special potion. [2] You will sleep for forty-two hours. Your family will think that you are dead. They will carry you to the tomb [3] of the Capulets. Meanwhile, I will send a message to Romeo. He will come secretly to the tomb. When you wake up, you can escape together. Are you brave enough to do this, Juliet?'

'Give me the bottle, Friar. Love will give me strength.'

Juliet went home. Lord and Lady Capulet were very happy when she told them that she had met Paris at Friar Laurence's cell and that she would marry him.

'Now I am going to my room to pray. Do not come with me, Nurse, I want to be alone.'

In her room, Juliet looked at the bottle of mysterious liquid which Friar Laurence had given her.

'I am afraid. Perhaps it is poison. Or perhaps I will wake in the tomb and

---

1. **weeping** : crying.
2. **potion** : a drink with a magical effect.
3. **tomb** : a place for the body of a dead person.

Romeo will not be there. I will be alone in the middle of all the dead bodies with my dead cousin, Tybalt. It will be terrible.'

Bravely, Juliet picked up the bottle and raised it to her lips.

'Romeo, Romeo, I drink to you!'

She drank. She fell on the bed and slept.

The next morning it was Thursday. The Nurse came to wake her up for her marriage. 'You lazy girl,' she said. 'You mustn't lie in bed on your wedding day... Help! Help! My lady's dead!'

Lord and Lady Capulet ran to their daughter's room.

'She's dead, she's dead, she's dead!' cried Lady Capulet.

'Her body is cold. I cannot speak,' said Lord Capulet.

At that moment, Paris and Friar Laurence entered the house. 'Is Juliet ready to go to the church?' asked the Friar.

'Oh Paris!' said Lord Capulet, 'Death has taken your wife.'

The Nurse began to cry. 'O terrible day! O sad day! O horrible day! There has never been such a black day. O sad day! O unhappy day!'

'Do not be sad,' said the Friar. 'Juliet is in Heaven. She's happier there than when she was alive.'

'The wedding must become a funeral,' [1] said Lord Capulet. 'Tell the musicians to play sad tunes. [2] Put the wedding flowers on my daughter's body.'

Lord and Lady Capulet took Juliet to the tomb of the Capulets. The Nurse, Lord Paris and Friar Laurence followed her body. The Friar was the only one who knew the secret — Juliet was alive. He was thinking, 'I have sent Friar John to Mantua to tell Romeo to come back to Verona. He will be here when Juliet wakes up.'

1. **funeral** : the event that happens when a dead person is buried or burnt.
2. **tunes** : music.

Go back to the text

1 Comprehension check
Answer the questions.

1   When did Lady Capulet go to Juliet's bedroom?
2   What did Lord Capulet think of Lord Paris?
3   What did the Nurse tell Juliet to do?
4   How long will Juliet sleep after drinking the potion?
5   Why didn't Juliet want the Nurse to stay with her?
6   Why did Friar Laurence send Friar John to Mantua?

2 Questions with *Who*
A   Write questions beginning with *Who*. Use the words in brackets. Remember, if *Who* is the subject of the verb, you don't need to use *did* in the question (e.g. Who loved Romeo?). If *Who* is the object, you do need to use *did* (e.g. Who did Juliet love?).

1   (visit Juliet in her bedroom?) Her mother did.
2   (kill Juliet's cousin?) Romeo did.
3   (Juliet ask for advice?) The Nurse and Friar Laurence.
4   (Juliet meet in Friar Laurence's cell?) Paris.
5   (find Juliet's body?) The Nurse did.
6   (Friar Laurence send to Mantua?) Friar John

B   Now write two more questions about *Romeo and Juliet*. Write one question with *Who* as the subject of the verb, and one question with *Who* as the object of the verb. Ask your questions to other members of the class.

C   In small groups, write 2-4 questions about history beginning with *Who*. Ask your questions to other members of the class.

3 Discussion
Work with a partner. Discuss the questions.

1   What do you think of Juliet's parents? Do they really care about her happiness?
2   The Nurse helped Romeo and Juliet to spend their wedding night together. Now she tells Juliet to forget Romeo and marry Paris. Why, do you think?
3   Friar Laurence married the young lovers because he wants to see peace in the city. Will there be peace if his plan succeeds?

'When her parents had gone, Juliet asked the Nurse for advice.'

Look at this sentence from Part Five.
When her parents **had gone**, *Juliet* **asked** *the Nurse for advice.*

There are two actions in the past — *had gone* and *asked*.
We use the Past Perfect form for the earlier action, *had gone*, and the Past Simple for the later action, *asked*.

Here is another example from Part Five.

In her room, Juliet **looked** *at the bottle of mysterious liquid which Friar Laurence* **had given** *her.*

4 **Past Perfect and Past Simple**

Put the verbs in brackets into the correct form - Past Perfect or Past Simple.

1   Romeo .... (*be*) in love with other girls before he .... (*meet*) Juliet.

2   Romeo .... (*tell*) Benvolio that he .... (*forget*) Rosaline.

3   Benvolio .... (*be*) worried because Tybalt .... (*challenge*) Romeo to fight.

4   Mercutio .... (*say*) that the Prince of Cats .... (*kill*) him.

5   The Prince .... (*send*) Romeo away because he .... (*kill*) Tybalt.

6   Paris .... (*not know*) that Juliet .... (*marry*) Romeo.

7   Juliet .... (*never be*) in love until she .... (*meet*) Romeo.

8   Juliet .... (*drink*) the potion that the Friar .... (*prepare*) for her.

9   Lord and Lady Capulet .... (*not understand*) why Juliet .... (*refuse*) to marry Paris.

10 After the Nurse .... (*dress*) Juliet in her wedding dress, Lord and Lady Capulet .... (*take*) her body to the family tomb.

Vocabulary — uncountable nouns

Uncountable nouns (for example: *sleep, literature, gold*)
•   don't usually have a plural form
•   are used with a singular verb
•   aren't used with a/an

5 Uncountable nouns

A **Look at these pairs of sentences. They all contain an uncountable noun. Only one of the sentences in each pair is correct. Put a tick in the box next to the correct sentence.**

1 A ☐ Juliet asked the Nurse for advices.
   B ☐ Juliet asked the Nurse for some advice.

2 A ☐ The news were terrible. Romeo and Juliet were dead.
   B ☐ The news was terrible. Romeo and Juliet were dead..

3 A ☐ Friar Laurence had a work to do in his garden.
   B ☐ Friar Laurence had work to do in his garden.

4 A ☐ Juliet saw bad luck in the future for her and Romeo.
   B ☐ Juliet saw a bad luck in the future for her and Romeo.

5 A ☐ Musicians played some sad music at Juliet's funeral.
   B ☐ Musicians played a sad music at Juliet's funeral.

B **Some uncountable nouns in English are often countable in other languages. Think about your language. Are the following nouns countable or uncountable?**

advice   information   furniture   progress

homework   luggage   money   news   hair

6 Vocabulary

We often use the phrase a ... of with uncountable nouns. Complete the a ... of phrases in these sentences with the following words.

piece   carton   bottle   jar   tube   bar   glass   cup

1 Julia gave me this .... of strawberry jam.
2 Would you like a .... of coffee?
3 Bring a .... of mineral water with you?
4 Could I have a .... of paper, please?
5 I feel sick! I've just eaten a big ...... of chocolate!
6 Can you get me a .... of orange juice from the supermarket?
7 I must remember to buy a .... of glue when I go to the stationer's.
8 When I was a child, I always had a ..... of hot milk at bedtime.

PET ⑦ Notices

Look at the text in each question. What does it say?
Mark the letter next to the correct explanation — A, B or C.

0

NO STREET FIGHTS AT ANY TIME

A ✓ You must never fight in the streets.
B ☐ You can fight in the streets sometimes.
C ☐ You can fight but not in the streets.

1

POISONOUS LIQUID
KEEP AWAY
FROM CHILDREN!!!

A ☐ Adults but not children may drink this.
B ☐ Only drink this when you are far away from children.
C ☐ You shouldn't let children have access to this liquid.

2

Guests for the wedding of Juliet Capulet and Lord Paris should be at the church by noon.

A ☐ No guests should arrive before noon.
B ☐ The wedding will start at noon or soon afterwards.
C ☐ The wedding will be finished before noon.

3

Come to the convent within an hour of receiving this message.

A ☐ You should come to the convent soon after you get this message.
B ☐ You should wait for an hour before coming to the convent.
C ☐ You can come to the convent at any time.

4

To: Friar-John@saintmarks
From: Friar Laurence
Subject: Padua Journey

Cancel your journey to Padua tomorrow and start for Mantua today to warn Romeo.

Friar John should
A ☐ go to Mantua today and Padua tomorrow.
B ☐ start his journey from Mantua.
C ☐ change the date and destination of his journey.

5

DANGER!!!
THIS AREA IS CLOSED
TO THE PUBLIC
FOR AT LEAST FOUR WEEKS
BECAUSE OF THE RISK
OF PLAGUE.

A ☐ The area will be safe after four weeks.
B ☐ You cannot enter this area.
C ☐ Be careful: if you enter this area, you may catch the plague.

11 **8** Listening

You will hear twelve statements about the story repeated twice. ELEVEN of them are not completely true. For these, write down a corrected version. But be careful! ONE of the statements is true.

For example, if you hear: *Romeo was Mercutio's brother.*
write: Romeo was Mercutio's **friend**.

1 ....

2 ....

3 ....

4 ....

5 ....

6 ....

7 ....

8 ....

9 ....

10 ....

11 ....

12 ....

T: GRADE 5

9 Speaking: music

Discuss the following questions with a partner.

1 Why do people listen to music?

2 What kind of music do you listen to when you feel sad? When you feel happy? When you're studying?

3 If you can play an instrument, tell your partner what you play, when you started, how often you practise, if you perform in public, and why you enjoy playing.

   If you don't play an instrument, tell your partner which instruments you like listening to and which you don't like listening to.

4 Everyone should study music and learn to play an instrument. Do you agree?

PET **10** Writing

This is part of a letter that you receive from a friend in another country.

> *In my country, people under 21 can't marry without the agreement of their parents. You can't get a driving licence or drink alcohol until you're 20. What rights do teenagers have in your country?*

Reply to this letter. Write your letter in about 100 words.

11 **Marriage**

Read the passage and fill in the gaps with the prepositions below. You need to use some prepositions more than once.

at   about (x2)   among (x2)   between   by   for (x2)
in (x4)   of (x4)   to (x2)   without

Rich, important families **(1)** .... 16th century England believed that marriage was **(2)** .... business rather than love. Parents chose future husbands and wives **(3)** .... their children, and families usually exchanged **(4)** .... money or property. The head **(5)** .... each family was almost always a man, and according **(6)** .... the law his wife and children had to obey him. So Juliet is extremely unusual — and extremely brave — when she chooses to marry **(7)** .... love and not to obey her parents, especially when they start to shout **(8)** .... her so violently.
These arranged marriages — that is, marriages where partners were chosen **(9)** .... parents — were much less common **(10)** .... the poor, because there was no economic advantage **(11)** .... a marriage **(12)** .... two poor people. So, at least the poor could fall **(13)** .... love and marry the person they loved.
Arranged marriages were not unusual **(14)** .... very rich European families even **(15)** .... the twentieth century, although a certain amount **(16)** .... choice was allowed **(17)** .... the young people involved. Members **(18)** .... royal families have started only recently to choose their partners, **(19)** .... needing to think too much **(20)** .... the political or social effects the marriage will have.

12 **Discussion**

Many young people in the world today think that a kind of arranged marriage, where the parents make plans but the children are consulted, is a good idea. Think of reasons for this. Check your ideas by asking someone who comes from a cultural tradition of arranged marriages, or in reference books or on the Internet.

Before you read

1 **Who do you think says...**

1   'I will ride to Verona tonight.'?
2   'Sweet Juliet, I will visit your grave every night and cry for you.'?
3   'With a kiss, I die.'?
4   'Quick, here is Romeo's dagger. Let me die.'?
5   'This is a terrible day for Verona.'?

Now read and listen to Part Six and check your ideas.

With a Kiss, I Die

omeo was in the city of Mantua.

'I have been dreaming about Juliet. I was dead but when she kissed me I became a king. Even a dream of love is sweet. This dream has made me happy.'

At that moment, his servant Balthasar found him. He had come with the latest news from Verona.

'Balthasar! What is the news from Verona? Have you got letters from the Friar? How is my mother? How is my father? How is Juliet?'

His servant replied sadly, 'Juliet is dead. She lies in the tomb of the Capulets.'

'What! Get me some horses! I will ride to Verona tonight.'

When Balthasar had gone, Romeo made his plans. 'I will go to the tomb. I will kiss her for the last time. Then I will drink poison. If Juliet is dead, I will die too.' He began to think carefully. 'There is an apothecary [1] who has a shop near here. He is very poor. If I pay him well, he will sell me some poison.'

---

1. **apothecary** : like a modern chemist or pharmacist, a person who sells medicines.

So Romeo went to the apothecary and gave him some gold.

'Here is the poison. It is enough to kill twenty men.'

In the middle of the night, Paris was at the tomb of the Capulets. He had come to put flowers on Juliet's grave.

'Sweet Juliet,' said Paris, 'I will visit your grave every night and cry for you. But someone is coming. I will hide and watch...'

Romeo arrived at the tomb with his servant. 'Give this letter to my father tomorrow morning, Balthasar. Now go away. Don't try to stop me. I am stronger than tigers or the roaring¹ sea.'

Romeo used a strong metal bar² to open the tomb. Paris was watching. 'This is Romeo, who murdered Juliet's cousin. He has come here to damage the tomb. I will arrest him!'

Paris called to Romeo. 'You are a Montague, the one who killed Tybalt. You must die!'

'I do not know you,' said Romeo. 'Go away if you want to live. Do not fight with me. I am desperate.'

'I arrest you, murderer!' said Paris.

They began to fight.

Romeo fought like a madman. He was stronger than Paris and killed him.

'Put my body with Juliet,' cried Paris as he died.

Romeo knelt down³ to look at his face.

'It is Paris! Balthasar told me that he wanted to marry Juliet. We are both unlucky. But where is Juliet? I must look at her beauty for the last time.'

---

1. **roaring** : making a loud noise like a lion or tiger.

2. **a metal bar** : a long piece of metal.

3. **knelt down** : went down on his knees.

Romeo and Juliet

Romeo went inside the tomb. He saw Juliet lying there and thought that she was dead.

'Oh my love, my wife! Death has kissed you. But you are still beautiful. Death is jealous. He keeps [1] you here as his lover. I will also stay here. But let me hold you in my arms. I love you.'

Romeo held Juliet. He took the bottle of poison out of his pocket and raised it to his lips.

Outside, someone was calling him, 'Romeo! Romeo!'

He kissed Juliet. 'With a kiss, I die.'

Meanwhile, Friar John had come to Friar Laurence's cell.

'Have you given my letter to Romeo, Friar John?'

'No, Friar Laurence. I did not reach [2] Mantua. There was plague [3] in one of the villages on the road and the soldiers didn't let me pass.'

'What! This is bad news. If Juliet wakes when Romeo is not there, she will be afraid. I must go to her.'

Friar Laurence hurried [4] to the tomb. He met Balthasar.

'I can see a light in the tomb. Who is looking among the skulls [5] and the worms?' [6]

'It is my master, Romeo.'

'How long has he been there?'

'Half an hour. I was sleeping but I dreamt there was a fight between my master and another man.'

'I must go to him. Romeo! Romeo!'

But when the Friar went inside the tomb, Romeo had already drunk the poison. He was dead.

Inside the tomb, it was cold and dark. Juliet woke up and saw the Friar.

'Where is Romeo?' she asked.

'He is dead,' replied the Friar. 'Paris is also dead. But we must go. The

1. **keeps** : makes you stay.
2. **reach** : arrive at.
3. **plague** : a very serious illness that affects other people quickly.
4. **hurried** : went quickly.
5. **skull** : bone of the head.   6. **worms** :

Watchman [1] is coming. Come with me. I will take you to the nuns, [2] who will let you live with them.'

'No, I will stay with Romeo,' said Juliet.

The Friar left her. Juliet held Romeo in her arms.

'I will drink poison too — but the bottle is empty. Let me kiss his lips. They are still warm. But I can hear people coming.'

Outside the tomb, the Watchman was approaching.

'Quick, here is Romeo's dagger. Let me die!'

Juliet stabbed [3] herself and fell.

Everyone arrived at the tomb of the Capulets. It was too late. Romeo and Juliet had both died. Their great love story was finished.

'Here is the body of Paris,' said the Watchman. 'And here are the bodies of a boy and girl.'

'Juliet!' cried Lord Capulet. 'There is blood and a dagger. Our only daughter is dead. This is a terrible day for the Capulets.'

Lord Montague spoke. 'Last night, my wife died from a broken heart because Romeo was banished from Verona. Now *he* is dead, poisoned. This is a terrible day for the Montagues.'

'I can explain everything,' said the Friar. 'It is all a mistake, a terrible mistake. They loved each other. The Nurse and I helped them to get married secretly. Now they are dead.'

Finally the Prince spoke.

'My friends Mercutio and Paris are dead. Tybalt is dead. Romeo and Juliet are dead. This is a terrible day for Verona. Lord Montague and Lord Capulet, shake hands. Your families must be friends. Love will change the world!'

1. **Watchman** : a kind of policeman.

2. **nuns** : women who live together in a religious community.

3. **stabbed** : killed with a knife.

Go back to the text

1 Comprehension check
Answer the questions.

1 What did Romeo decide to do?
2 Why did Paris want to fight Romeo?
3 Was Juliet really dead when Romeo saw her?
4 Why didn't Friar Laurence's plan succeed?
5 How did Juliet kill herself?
6 How many people are dead at the end of the story? Who are they?

2 Characters
Here are some opinions about the characters in the play. If you agree, put a tick in the box under 'A'. If you disagree, put a tick in the box under 'D'. If you aren't sure, put a tick in the box under '?'. Compare your answers with your partner's.

		A	D	?
1	Romeo and Juliet were too young to love.	☐	☐	☐
2	Lord and Lady Capulet were bad parents.	☐	☐	☐
3	The Prince was a weak governor.	☐	☐	☐
4	Paris didn't love Juliet as much as Romeo did.	☐	☐	☐
5	Romeo was a murderer.	☐	☐	☐
6	Juliet was right to kill herself.	☐	☐	☐
7	Friar Laurence was wrong to marry Romeo and Juliet.	☐	☐	☐
8	Tybalt was the worst person in the story.	☐	☐	☐
9	Benvolio was the best person in the story.	☐	☐	☐
10	The Nurse was a foolish old woman.	☐	☐	☐

3 Discussion
Discuss these questions with a partner.

1 Romeo and Juliet were not very lucky lovers. How were they unlucky?
2 Who is responsible for the deaths of Romeo and Juliet? Their parents? Friar Laurence? Tybalt? All of them? None of them?

'Romeo was banished to Mantua.'

Look at these 2 sentences.

a *The Prince **banished** Romeo to Mantua.* (Past Simple Active)

b *Romeo **was banished** to Mantua by the Prince.* (Past Simple Passive)

We choose the active or the passive to change the focus of attention. In sentence **a** we make the Prince more important, while in sentence **b** we make Romeo more important.

4 Past Simple Passive

Rewrite these sentences in the Past Simple Passive. Use *was* or *were* + the past participle.

1 The Capulet servants started the fight.
   ....

2 Lord Capulet invited a lot of important people to the party.
   ....

3 The Scaligeri family ruled Verona for more than a century.
   ....

4 Tybalt challenged Romeo to a fight.
   ....

5 Romeo killed Tybalt.
   ....

6 Friar Laurence married Romeo and Juliet.
   ....

7 The Nurse found Juliet's body.
   ....

8 Some servants took Juliet's body to the tomb.
   ....

9 William Shakespeare wrote the play *Romeo and Juliet*.
   ....

5 Vocabulary – suffixes for making nouns: *-tion* & *-ness*
Complete the table.

NOUN	VERB	NOUN	ADJECTIVE
separation	separate	happiness	happy
....	explain	....	kind
....	prepare	....	sad
....	invite	....	lazy

PET **6** **Fill in the gaps**

Read the text below, which is in the form of a newspaper article, and choose the correct word for each space. For each question, mark the letter next to the correct word — A, B, C or D.

TRAGIC DEATH OF TWO YOUNG LOVERS

The bodies (**0**) ..A...... three people (**1**) .... found at the tomb of the Capulet family in the early hours of this morning. A watchman discovered the body of Lord Paris, a close friend of the prince of Verona, (**2**) .... the door of the tomb. Inside, there was an even (**3**) .... sight. Juliet of the Capulets and Romeo of the Montagues lay dead on the ground. Next to the boy's body (**4**) .... was a bottle which had contained poison. The girl (**5**) .... killed herself with the boy's dagger. Later, a friend of the young couple, Friar Laurence, explained (**6**) .... had happened. The two teenagers met at a party that Lord Capulet had given and fell in love. (**7**) .... they were both very young, they decided to get married. They couldn't tell their parents because the families were enemies. Friar Laurence married (**8**) .... secretly because he hoped the marriage would bring peace to the city of Verona. (**9**) .... the girl's parents ordered her to marry Lord Paris, she didn't know what to do. Then, to (**10**) .... things worse, Romeo killed her cousin in a fight. The Prince of Verona has promised a full investigation into the tragic fate of these two young people, who he defined as 'star-crossed lovers'.

0	Ⓐ of	B at	C in	D by
1	A have	B had	C are	D were
2	A next	B over	C near	D in
3	A bad	B worse	C worst	D badly
4	A it	B this	C that	D there
5	A was	B had	C did	D has
6	A it	B why	C that	D what
7	A But	B So	C Because	D Although
8	A they	B their	C themselves	D them
9	A As	B When	C Until	D Before
10	A have	B turn	C make	D do

 INTERNET PROJECT

Connect to the Internet and go to www.blackcat-cideb.com or www.cideb.it. Insert the title or part of the title of the book into our search engine. Open the page for *Romeo and Juliet*. Click on the Internet project link. Go down the page until you find the title of this book and click on the relevant link for this project.

▶ Who was Tristan? Where was he from?   ▶ When did they live?

▶ Who was Isolde? Where was she from?   ▶ Why was their love story sad?

Discuss your answers with the class.

7 **O Romeo, Romeo, wherefore art thou Romeo?**

You will hear some famous lines from Shakespeare's original play. Remember that Shakespeare wrote 400 years ago so the language is different from modern English. Which character is speaking and at what point in the story? Discuss your ideas with a partner.

A .... : Thou * wast the prettiest babe that e'r I nursed.
An I might live to see thee * married once, I have my wish.
* ***Thou, thee, thy:*** *old forms of 'you, you and your'.*

B .... : For you and I are past our dancing days.

C .... : It seems she hangs upon the cheek * of night
As a rich jewel in an Ethiop's ear.
* ***cheek:*** *the side of the face.*

D .... : My only love sprung* from my only hate!
* ***sprung:*** *(past participle of 'to spring') come from.*

E .... : But soft, what light through yonder * window breaks?
It is the east, and Juliet is the sun.
* ***yonder:*** *that.*

F .... : See how she leans her cheek upon her hand.
O, that I were a glove upon that hand,
That I might touch that cheek!

G .... : O Romeo, Romeo, wherefore art thou * Romeo?
Deny thy father and refuse thy name,
* ***Wherefore art thou:*** *Why are you called...*

H .... : What's in a name? That which we call a rose
By any other word would smell as sweet.

I .... : O, swear * not by the moon, th'inconstant moon *
* ***swear:*** *promise seriously.*
* ***th'inconstant moon:*** *the changeable moon.*

J .... : Good night, good night. Parting is such sweet sorrow
That I shall say good night till it be morrow.

K .... : Young men's love then lies
Not truly in their hearts, but in their eyes.

L .... : A plague o' both your houses.*
They have made worms' meat of me.
* ***houses:*** *(here) families.*

M .... : For never was a story of more woe *
Than this of Juliet and her Romeo.
* ***woe:*** *sadness.*

Romeo and Juliet on Film

There had been some silent films of Shakespeare's play, but the 1936 film of *Romeo and Juliet* was a Hollywood blockbuster. [1] Many people thought the actors playing the lovers were too old: Leslie Howard as Romeo was forty-three and Norma Shearer as Juliet was thirty-four. But a lot of people who never went to the theatre saw *Romeo and Juliet* for the first time at the cinema.

Leonardo di Caprio and Claire Danes in Baz Luhrmann's **Romeo + Juliet** fall in love at the party (see Part Two). They have costumes, but not masks!

West Side Story (1961) is a film version of the 1959 stage musical. [2] It won an Oscar for best film. The setting is New York in the 1950s; Tony (Romeo) is a member of the 'Sharks', a gang [3] of young people originally from Eastern Europe, while Maria (Juliet) is from the 'Jets', a gang of young people originally from Puerto

1. **blockbuster** : an extremely popular and successful film or book; it makes a lot of money.
2. **musical** : a play or film that uses singing and dancing in the story.
3. **gang** : a group of people (often young) who often do things that are against the law.

In this scene from the film **West Side Story**, the girl members of the Jets make fun of the boys. They like their new life in New York, but the boys want to go back to Puerto Rico. Is it easier for girls to adapt than boys?

Rico. The music, by the American composer Leonard Bernstein, includes classical and Latin American styles, and the words by Stephen Sondheim are both funny and moving.

The Italian director Franco Zeffirelli set his *Romeo and Juliet* (1968) in medieval Italy. He filmed scenes in Italian towns in Tuscany and Umbria, and the film won an Oscar for best costumes. [1] Two young actors played the lovers: Leonard Whiting was eighteen and Olivia Hussey was sixteen.

The Australian director Baz Luhrmann also used two young actors for his *Romeo + Juliet* (1997): Leonardo di Caprio was twenty-one and Claire Danes was sixteen. But the setting – 'Verona Beach' – is a fictional Californian town, a swimming pool is used for the 'balcony scene', and the actors speak Shakespeare's text with American accents.

1. **costumes** : clothes worn in a play or film that are typical of a historical time.

The blockbuster *Titanic* (1997) won Oscars for best film and best director (James Cameron). Of course, it is not Shakespeare's play! But the story is very similar: two young people (the boy is played by Leonardo di Caprio again!) from different backgrounds [1] fall in love, but after a few days their love ends in death.

A lot of films, not only *Titanic*, have used Shakespeare's *Romeo and Juliet*.

Shakespeare in Love (1999) won Oscars for best film and best actress (Gwyneth Paltrow). The story – completely fictional! – is about Shakespeare falling in love and writing *Romeo and Juliet*. It gives a good idea of the Elizabethan theatre; it shows how boy actors played female parts, such as Juliet, because women were not allowed to act in the theatres.

1 Comprehension check
Which of the six films described above

1   has/have a lot of songs and dancing?
2   is/are not films of Shakespeare's *Romeo and Juliet*?
3   has/have young actors playing *Romeo and Juliet*?
4   has/have older actors playing *Romeo and Juliet*?
5   gives/give a good idea of the Elizabethan theatre?
6   was/were filmed in Italy?
7   has/have modern settings?
8   won Oscars?

2 On your own or in pairs, make a question about the films to ask other students in the class.

3 Discussion
1   Have you seen any of these films? If so, what is your opinion?
2   Which film(s) would you like to see, and why?

---

1.   **backgrounds** : your background is your family and your education. It includes race, religion and if you are rich or poor.

Great Love Stories

In the left-hand column there is a list, a-h, of elements of great love stories. In column 1 you can see that *Romeo and Juliet* has all of these elements.

Work in pairs or groups. What do you know about other great love stories? Choose one classic love story from the past (perhaps from your own culture) and one contemporary love story (perhaps a film, or even a true story). Write the titles (or the lovers' names) in columns 2 and 3. Now complete columns 2 and 3 with yes or no, to show whether the stories have the elements a-h or not.

Elements of great love stories	1. *Romeo and Juliet*	2.	3.	4.
a The story ends with the death of one or both of the lovers.	Yes (both)			
b One or both of the lovers falls in love at first sight, or in a very short time.	Yes			
c Their love is 'impossible': it must stay a secret.	Yes (the feud)			
d The lovers are very young and good-looking.	Yes			
e The lovers have a very short period of happiness before something terrible happens.	Yes (a few days)			
f One of the lovers has had a previous experience of love which was not satisfactory.	Yes (Romeo)			
g The woman says she is in love first.	Yes			
h Most of the lovers' meetings take place in secret.	Yes			

Which of the elements a-h are most important in tragic love stories? Number them from 1 (the most important) to 8 (the least important) in column 4. Compare your ideas in class. Why do you think *Romeo and Juliet* has become the most famous love story in the Western world – the classic love story?

PET ① Comprehension check

Look at the sentences below.

Decide if each sentence is correct or incorrect. If it is correct, mark A. If it is not correct, mark B.

		A	B
1	Juliet was a Capulet and Romeo was a Montague.	☐	☐
2	First of all, Juliet's parents wanted her to marry Tybalt.	☐	☐
3	Juliet's father wanted Tybalt to fight Romeo.	☐	☐
4	The Nurse discovered Juliet talking to Romeo from the balcony.	☐	☐
5	Friar Laurence agreed to help them because he wanted peace.	☐	☐
6	Mercutio fought Tybalt after Romeo had refused the challenge.	☐	☐
7	Romeo visited Juliet for the last time with the Nurse's help.	☐	☐
8	The Nurse advised Juliet to forget Romeo and marry Paris.	☐	☐
9	Paris fought Romeo because he had married Juliet secretly.	☐	☐
10	When the Friar arrived at the tomb, both lovers were dead.	☐	☐

Now rewrite the incorrect sentences.

PET ② Fill in the gaps

Read the text below and choose the correct word for each space. For each question, mark the letter next to the correct word — A, B, C or D.

(0) ..A...... love bring happiness? Romeo and Juliet (1) .... in love as soon as they saw each other. In other (2) ...., it was love at first (3) .... Usually, falling in love is a very happy experience that (4) .... lead to marriage and a lifetime together. (5) ...., in this case, the love of the teenage couple caused a series of problems. Mercutio, Tybalt and Paris all (6) .... In addition Romeo and Juliet killed (7) .... as a result of a terrible misunderstanding. (8) .... was responsible? Was it Friar Laurence or their parents or Tybalt? What (9) .... you (10) .... ?

0	Ⓐ Does	B Do	C Why	D Is
1	A fell	B were	C felt	D fallen
2	A terms	B words	C wise	D example
3	A seeing	B look	C sight	D glance
4	A maybe	B may	C have	D does
5	A Although	B And	C However	D Also
6	A dead	B death	C dyed	D died

7	**A** them	**B** they	**C** their	**D** themselves
8	**A** What	**B** How	**C** Which	**D** Who
9	**A** do	**B** are	**C** does	**D** have
10	**A** thinking	**B** thought	**C** think	**D** agree

PET ③ Comprehension check

These questions are about the whole story. For each question, mark the letter next to the best answer — A, B, C or D.

1 What is our main impression of Romeo?

   A ☐ He was clever and thoughtful.

   B ☐ Juliet was the only girl he ever loved.

   C ☐ He sometimes acted too quickly without thinking.

   D ☐ He defended his own family passionately.

2 Friar Laurence

   A ☐ tried to help Romeo and Juliet but failed.

   B ☐ gave poison to Juliet.

   C ☐ acted kindly and openly most of the time.

   D ☐ didn't like the Montagues and Capulets.

3 The Prince banished Romeo

   A ☐ because it is wrong to kill.

   B ☐ because he married Juliet without permission.

   C ☐ because he was a Montague.

   D ☐ because he didn't know what else to do.

4 Which of the following is the best overall description of the story of *Romeo and Juliet*?

   A ☐ Two teenage lovers overcome their problems despite the disapproval of their parents.

   B ☐ Two teenage lovers die as a result of a secret plan that went wrong.

   C ☐ The love between two teenagers ends in death because of the feud between their families.

   D ☐ Two families end their long-standing quarrel as a result of a secret marriage between their children.

Key to Exit Test

1   1A, 2B, 3B, 4B, 5A, 6A, 7A, 8A, 9B, 10 B

2   1A, 2B, 3C, 4B, 5C, 6D, 7D, 8D, 9A, 10 C

3   1C, 2A, 3A, 4 C

Romeo and Juliet

Playscript

The Montagues and the Capulets

In the beautiful city of Verona, there are two families — the Montagues and the Capulets. They hate each other. They have hated each other for hundreds of years. One day, the servants begin to fight in the streets.

SERVANTS OF THE MONTAGUES : The Montagues are better than the Capulets!

SERVANTS OF THE CAPULETS : Our masters, the Capulets, are better!

Then Benvolio and Tybalt arrive.

BENVOLIO : Stop fighting!

TYBALT : Fight with me, Benvolio.

BENVOLIO : No! Fighting is stupid!

TYBALT : Your sword is out. Fight!

Then Lord and Lady Capulet arrive. Lord Capulet is old but he wants to fight too.

LORD CAPULET : Bring me my sword.

LADY CAPULET : You're too old to fight. You don't need a sword,
    you need a crutch.

Then Lord and Lady Montague arrive. Soon everyone is fighting. It is very dangerous. At last, the Prince arrives. He is very angry.

PRINCE : Stop fighting! I want peace in my city.
    Lord Capulet and Lord Montague, you are old but you are not wise. If your two
    families fight again, you will both die!

LORD CAPULET : I, Lord Capulet, promise not to fight again.

LORD MONTAGUE : I, Lord Montague, promise not to fight again.

The Prince is happy. Everyone goes away.

PAUSE

Lady Montague and Benvolio are talking.

BENVOLIO : Tybalt wants to kill all the Montagues. He's very dangerous.

LADY MONTAGUE : Where is my son, Romeo? Is he safe?

BENVOLIO : He's not here. He's walking by himself in the forest. He's sad.

LADY MONTAGUE : Why is he sad?

BENVOLIO : I don't know. But look, he's coming now. I'll ask him.
    Why are you unhappy, Romeo?

ROMEO : I am in love.

BENVOLIO : Who do you love?

ROMEO : I love sweet Rosaline. She is beautiful, intelligent and good. But she doesn't
    love me. That is why I'm sad.

BENVOLIO : Forget her. There are many other girls.

ROMEO : No, I can never forget her.

PAUSE

Lord Capulet is talking to his wife, Lady Capulet.

LORD CAPULET : I'm going to have a party. I'll invite all the important people from
    Verona. But not the Montagues.

LADY CAPULET : You must invite Paris.

LORD CAPULET : Yes, I want him to meet Juliet. One day, they will get married.

LADY CAPULET : I like that idea. I'll go and tell Juliet.

LORD CAPULET : Tell my servant to come here.

SERVANT : Yes, my Lord?

LORD CAPULET : Here is a list of guests. Go and invite them.

*The servant meets Romeo and Benvolio in the street. He does not know that they are
Montagues.*

SERVANT : Can you help me? I can't read the names on this piece of paper.

BENVOLIO : Look, Romeo. Rosaline will be at the party.

ROMEO : I have an idea.

PAUSE

Lady Capulet is talking to Juliet. Juliet is nearly fourteen years old. She has an old nurse who looks after her.

LADY CAPULET : You will meet Paris at the party. Perhaps you will marry him one day.

JULIET : Mother, I'm too young to get married.

NURSE : I would love to see my little Juliet married. You will have happy days and happy nights.

SERVANT : The party is ready, my lady.

ACT **TWO**
The Garden of the Capulets

Romeo is going to the party with Benvolio and his friend, Mercutio. They are all wearing masks. It is very dangerous for the Montagues and their friends to go to a party in the house of the Capulets.

ROMEO : Put on your masks. They mustn't recognise us. I can't wait to see fair Rosaline.

SERVANT : Welcome, gentlemen. Come in. Dance and drink and eat. Enjoy yourselves.

As they go into the house, Romeo sees Juliet for the first time.
He forgets Rosaline! He falls in love! But Tybalt recognises Romeo's voice.

ROMEO : Who's that lady? She's more beautiful than the moon. I have never loved until now.

TYBALT : I know his voice. It's a Montague. I'll kill him.

LORD CAPULET : Be calm, Tybalt. This is a party. I want no trouble.

Romeo goes to Juliet and talks to her. He does not know who she is.

ROMEO : My lips are ready to kiss you.

JULIET : But I don't know you.

ROMEO : I must kiss you.

JULIET : Here I am. My lips are here.

Romeo kisses Juliet. He kisses her a second time.

NURSE : Juliet, your mother wants you. You must come with me.

ROMEO : Excuse me, who's that girl?

NURSE : Young man, that is Juliet. She's a Capulet.

ROMEO : *(thinking aloud)* What! I'm in love with the daughter of the enemy of my family.

JULIET : Nurse, who's that young man?

NURSE : That is Romeo. He's a Montague.

JULIET : Oh no! I'm in love with the son of the enemy of my family. We can never get married.

After they leave the party, Mercutio and Benvolio look for Romeo.

MERCUTIO : Look! He's there in the shadows. What's he doing?

BENVOLIO : He's jumping the wall. He's going into the garden of the Capulets.

MERCUTIO : Romeo! Madman! Lover! He's going to look for Rosaline.

BENVOLIO : Quiet! You'll make him angry. His love is blind.

MERCUTIO : Good night, Romeo. He's probably sitting under a tree, dreaming about that girl. He's mad.

Mercutio and Benvolio go home. The night is silent.

In the dark garden, Romeo suddenly sees a light. Juliet is standing on her balcony. She begins to speak to the night. She does not know that Romeo is listening.

JULIET : O Romeo, Romeo! Why is your name Romeo? Let's change our names. Then we can love. Forget that you're a Montague. Or, if you love me, I will not be a Capulet. Montague and Capulet are only names. A rose can have any name. It always smells sweet.

ROMEO : I will change my name for you.

JULIET : Who's there? Who's listening in the middle of the night?

ROMEO : It's me. Romeo.

JULIET : Why are you there?

ROMEO : I love you. And I know that you love me.

JULIET : What shall we do? Our families are enemies.

ROMEO : We must get married secretly. We will do it tomorrow. I'll tell the Nurse where you must meet me. Will you marry me?

JULIET : Yes, Romeo. But will you be true?

ROMEO : Yes, my darling.

NURSE : Juliet! Juliet!

JULIET : Good night, Romeo. I must go. The Nurse is calling.

ROMEO : Good night, Juliet.

NURSE : Juliet! Juliet!

JULIET : I'm coming, Nurse. Good night.

ROMEO : Good night.

JULIET : Good night.

ROMEO : (further away) Good night.

JULIET : It's very sad and very sweet to say good night. But tomorrow, we will be married.

ACT **THREE**
The Prince of Cats

Romeo goes to see Friar Laurence, his friend and teacher. The Friar is working in his garden. The sun is rising. It is a beautiful morning.

ROMEO : I want to get married.

FRIAR : To Rosaline?

ROMEO : No, to Juliet. I love her.

FRIAR : Good. Perhaps your marriage will make the Capulets and the Montagues friends. It's a good thing for Verona. I will help you.

Benvolio and Mercutio are looking for Romeo in the streets of Verona.

BENVOLIO : Poor Romeo. His heart is broken. Rosaline does not love him.

MERCUTIO : That's not his only problem. Tybalt has sent a letter to his house. He wants to fight him.

BENVOLIO : Tybalt is dangerous.

MERCUTIO : Yes. Tybalt is the Prince of Cats. He's an artist with his sword. Romeo is a lamb. He will die.

BENVOLIO : Quiet! Here comes Romeo.

ROMEO : Hello, Benvolio. Hello, Mercutio, my friend.

MERCUTIO : Are you still sad? Have you been crying all night for Rosaline? But look, here comes a fat old woman.

NURSE : Romeo, Romeo. I must talk with you, privately. Do you have any news for Juliet?

ROMEO : Yes. Tell Juliet to come to Friar Laurence's cell this afternoon. We'll get married there.

NURSE : I love Juliet, sir. I remember when she was a little child. Look after her when you are her husband.

The Nurse goes back to Juliet. She tells her the news. The two lovers get ready for their secret wedding. In the afternoon, the sun is shining. Romeo goes secretly to Friar Laurence's cell.

FRIAR : The day is bright. It's a sign that the future will be happy.

ROMEO : I don't care if I die tomorrow. It's enough that Juliet is mine.

FRIAR : Don't be so passionate. It's better to love moderately. Then love will last longer.

At last Juliet arrives. She is very nervous. So is Romeo. They are very young but very much in love. Friar Laurence is like a father to them. He takes them into his cell and they are married.

But in the streets of Verona, there are problems.

TYBALT : Mercutio, where is Romeo?

MERCUTIO : I don't know. Why?

TYBALT : I want to kill him. He came to the party of the Capulets. You're his friend. You came with him. I want to fight you too.

MERCUTIO : Here is Romeo.

TYBALT : Fight, you villain!

ROMEO : I cannot fight you.

MERCUTIO : Romeo! Are you a coward? Tybalt!

TYBALT : What do you want?

MERCUTIO : I want one of your nine lives, Prince of Cats!

TYBALT : I will fight you as Romeo is too afraid to fight.

ROMEO : Stop fighting. The Prince will be angry. He will punish you. Stop, Tybalt. Stop, good Mercutio!

MERCUTIO : Agh! I'm hurt. I'm dying. Romeo, this quarrel between your families has killed me.

Mercutio falls to the ground and dies. It is Romeo's fault. His friend is dead.

ACT **FOUR**
Fortune's Fool

Romeo is angry. He loses control. He takes out his sword and fights with Tybalt. He kills him.

ROMEO : He killed my friend. Now he's dead. He's with Mercutio.

BENVOLIO : Romeo, you must escape. The people are coming. The Prince will punish you with death...

ROMEO : Oh, I am Fortune's fool! I must go.

PRINCE : What's happening? How did Tybalt die?

BENVOLIO : Romeo wanted to stop the fight. But Tybalt killed Mercutio. Then Romeo killed Tybalt.

PRINCE : Romeo must leave Verona. He has murdered Tybalt. If I find him in Verona, he will die.

LADY CAPULET : Tybalt is dead. The Montagues must pay for this. Benvolio is lying. Romeo is a murderer and must die.

Juliet is waiting for Romeo, her new husband. She wants the night to come so that they can be together. But when the Nurse arrives, she brings bad news.

NURSE : He's dead!

JULIET : What? Is Romeo dead?

NURSE : No, Tybalt is dead. Romeo has killed him. He must leave Verona.

JULIET : Did Romeo kill my cousin? Then he's a villain. But I love him.

NURSE : Your father and mother are crying for Tybalt.

JULIET : I will cry for him too. But I will cry longer for Romeo. I will never see him again. I will kill myself.

NURSE : No. Romeo is hiding with Friar Laurence. I will bring him to you.

The Nurse comes to find Romeo. He is talking to Friar Laurence.

ROMEO : Everything is finished. I will kill myself with this knife.

FRIAR : No, be brave. You must go to Mantua. You will be safe there. I will send you news about Juliet. One day, you will be together again. But tonight, go with the Nurse. See Juliet for the last time.

NURSE : Come with me. Here is the house of the Capulets. Here's a ladder. Climb up and go through the window.

So Romeo spends his marriage night with Juliet.

Downstairs, in the house of the Capulets, Lord and Lady Capulet are talking. Lord Paris is with them.

LORD CAPULET : I will talk to Juliet. She will marry you next Thursday. Tybalt is dead. There must be something good for the Capulet family — Juliet's wedding! I am her father. She will do as I say. Wife, see Juliet in the morning and tell her. She will marry Paris.

In the morning, Romeo leaves Juliet. He must escape to Mantua before the Prince finds him.

JULIET : Must you go? It's still night. The nightingale is singing, not the lark.

ROMEO : Look at the sky. The sun is rising. But I want to stay.

JULIET : Go. It's dangerous for you here. But I want you to stay. Goodbye, sweet Romeo. Will I ever see you again?

ROMEO : Goodbye. I will think of you every second of the day.

My Lady's Dead!

Lady Capulet tells Juliet that she must marry Paris.

LADY CAPULET : You will get married to Paris early next Thursday morning.

JULIET : No, Mother. As you know, I hate Romeo. He has killed my cousin. But I'd rather marry Romeo than Paris.

JULIET *(thinking)* : But I'm already married.

LORD CAPULET : Paris is a fine gentleman. Marry him on Thursday or never speak to me again.

NURSE : Please don't be angry with my little Juliet, sir.

LORD CAPULET : Shut up, you fat old fool. I have decided. If you don't obey me, I will throw you out in the streets. Goodbye. Remember, on Thursday you are going to be married.

LADY CAPULET : Goodbye, daughter. You must obey your father.

JULIET : Nurse, what should I do?

NURSE : Well, Romeo is not here. Paris is a fine gentleman, it's true. He's more handsome than Romeo. Forget Romeo and marry Paris.

JULIET : Do you speak from your heart? *(thinking)* I cannot trust her. I will ask the Friar for advice. He's the only person who can help me.

The Friar is very worried. He is talking to Paris.

PARIS : I am going to marry Juliet.

FRIAR : Does she love you?

PARIS : I don't know. We haven't talked about love because she's weeping for her cousin's death. But our marriage will make her happy again.

FRIAR : But look, here comes Juliet.

PARIS : Welcome, my lady and my wife. Have you come to tell the Friar that you love me?

JULIET : I can't answer that. But please, let me talk to the Friar privately.

PARIS : Goodbye. I know that you love me. I will see you on Thursday in the church.

FRIAR : Be happy, Juliet. I have a plan. You and Romeo will be together.

JULIET : Tell me! What is it?

FRIAR : Go home and agree to marry Paris. On Wednesday night, go to your bedroom alone. Take this bottle and drink the liquid. It is a special potion. You will sleep for forty-two hours. Your family will think that you are dead. They will carry you to the tomb of the Capulets. Meanwhile, I will send a message to Romeo. He will come secretly to the tomb. When you wake up, you can escape together. Are you brave enough to do this, Juliet?

JULIET : Give me the bottle, Friar. Love will give me strength.

Juliet goes home.

JULIET : Mother, Father, I have changed my mind. I will obey you. I have seen Lord Paris at the Friar's cell and I've told him that I love him.

LORD CAPULET : Good, you're a good daughter.

LADY CAPULET : You've made your old father happy.

JULIET : Now I'm going to my room to pray. Don't come with me, Nurse, I want to be alone.

PAUSE

JULIET : Here is the bottle. I am afraid. Perhaps it's poison. Or perhaps I will wake in the tomb and Romeo will not be there. I will be alone in the middle of all the dead bodies with my dead cousin, Tybalt. It will be terrible.

Bravely, Juliet picks up the bottle and raises it to her lips.

JULIET : Romeo, Romeo, I drink to you!

She drinks. She falls on the bed and sleeps...

The next morning it is Thursday. The Nurse comes to wake her up for her marriage.

NURSE : You lazy girl. Why are you still sleeping? You mustn't lie in bed on your wedding day.... . Help! Help! My lady's dead! My lady's dead!

Lord and Lady Capulet take Juliet to the tomb of the Capulets. They are very sad. Their only child is dead.

FRIAR : I have sent Friar John to Mantua to tell Romeo to come back to Verona. He will be here when Juliet wakes up.

NURSE : Oh sad day! Oh unhappy day! Oh terrible day!

ACT SIX
With a Kiss, I Die

Romeo is in Mantua. His servant, Balthasar, comes to bring him the latest news.

ROMEO : I have been dreaming about Juliet. Even a dream of love is sweet.

BALTHASAR : Juliet is dead.

ROMEO : What! I will ride to Verona tonight. I will kiss her for the last time. Then I will drink poison. If Juliet is dead, I will die too.

In the middle of the night, Romeo arrives at the tomb of the Capulets. Paris is also there with his servant.

PARIS : I have come to put flowers on Juliet's grave. But who is this? You're a Montague, the one who killed Tybalt. You must die.

ROMEO : I don't know you. Go away if you want to live. Don't fight with me. I'm desperate. I'm stronger than tigers or the roaring sea.

PARIS : I arrest you, murderer.

They fight.

ROMEO : It's Paris! I've killed him. Balthasar told me that he wanted to marry Juliet. We are both unlucky. But where is Juliet? I must look at her beauty for the last time.

PAUSE

ROMEO : Oh my love, my wife! Death has kissed you. But you're still beautiful. Death is jealous. He keeps you here as his lover. I will stay here too. But let me kiss you. With a kiss, I die.

Romeo kisses Juliet. He takes a bottle of poison out of his pocket and raises it to his lips.

FRIAR : Romeo! Romeo!

Friar John has come to Friar Laurence's cell.

FRIAR : Have you given my letter to Romeo, Friar John?

JOHN : No, Friar Laurence. I didn't reach Mantua. There was plague in one of the villages on the road and the soldiers didn't let me pass.

FRIAR : What! This is bad news. If Juliet wakes when Romeo isn't there, she will be afraid. I must go to her.

PAUSE

FRIAR : I can see a light in the tomb. Who's looking among the skulls and the worms?

BALTHASAR : It's my master, Romeo.

FRIAR : I must go to him. Romeo! Romeo!

But when the Friar goes inside the tomb, Romeo has already drunk the poison. He is dead.
Juliet wakes up and sees the Friar.

JULIET : Where is Romeo?

FRIAR : He's dead. We must go. The watchman is coming. Come with me.

JULIET : No, I will stay with Romeo. I will drink poison too — but the bottle is empty. Let me kiss his lips. They are still warm. I can hear people coming. Quick, here's Romeo's dagger. Let me die!

Everyone arrives at the tomb of the Capulets. It is too late. Romeo and Juliet have both died. Their great love story is finished.

WATCHMAN : Here is the body of Paris. And here are the bodies of a boy and girl...

LORD CAPULET : Juliet! There's blood and a dagger. Our only daughter is dead. This is a terrible day for the Capulets.

LORD MONTAGUE : Last night, my wife died from a broken heart because Romeo was banished from Verona. Now he's dead, poisoned. This is a terrible day for the Montagues.

FRIAR : I can explain everything. It's all a mistake, a terrible mistake. They loved each other. The Nurse and I helped them to get married secretly. Now they're dead.

PRINCE : My friends Mercutio and Paris are dead. Tybalt is dead. Romeo and Juliet are dead. This is a terrible day for Verona. Lord Montague and Lord Capulet, shake hands. Your families must be friends. Love will change the world.

This reader uses the **EXPANSIVE READING** approach, where the text becomes a springboard to improve language skills and to explore historical background, cultural connections and other topics suggested by the text.

The new structures introduced in this step of our **R**EADING & **T**RAINING series are listed below. Naturally, structures from lower steps are included too. For a complete list of structures used over all the six steps, see *The Black Cat Guide to Graded Readers*, which is also downloadable at no cost from our website, www.blackcat-cideb.com or www.cideb.it.

The vocabulary used at each step is carefully checked against vocabulary lists used for internationally recognised examinations.

Step Three B1.2

All the structures used in the previous levels, plus the following:

Verb tenses
Present Perfect Simple: unfinished past with
 for or *since* (duration form)
Past Perfect Simple: narrative

Verb forms and patterns
Regular verbs and all irregular verbs in current
 English
Causative: *have / get* + object + past participle
Reported questions and orders with *ask* and *tell*

Modal verbs
Would: hypothesis
Would rather: preference
Should (present and future reference):
 moral obligation
Ought to (present and future reference):
 moral obligation
Used to: past habits and states

Types of clause
2nd Conditional: *if* + past, *would(n't)*
Zero, 1st and 2nd conditionals with *unless*
Non-defining relative clauses with *who*
 and *where*
Clauses of result: *so*; *so ... that*; *such ... that*
Clauses of concession: *although, though*

Other
Comparison: *(not) as / so ... as*; *(not) ...*
 enough to; *too ... to*

Available at Step Three:

- **The £1,000,000 Banknote** Mark Twain
- **The Canterville Ghost** Oscar Wilde
- **Classic Detective Stories**
- **The Diamond as Big as The Ritz**
  F. Scott Fitzgerald
- **Great Mysteries of Our World**
  Gina D. B. Clemen
- **Gulliver's Travels** Jonathan Swift
- **The Hound of the Baskervilles**
  Sir Arthur Conan Doyle
- **Jane Eyre** Charlotte Brontë
- **Kim** Rudyard Kipling
- **Lord Arthur Savile's Crime**
  and Other Stories Oscar Wilde
- **Moonfleet** John Meade Falkner
- **Of Mice and Men** John Steinbeck
- **The Pearl** John Steinbeck
- **The Phantom of the Opera** Gaston Leroux
- **The Prisoner of Zenda** Anthony Hope
- **The Return of Sherlock Holmes**
  Sir Arthur Conan Doyle
- **The Scarlet Pimpernel** Baroness Orczy
- **Sherlock Holmes Investigates**
  Sir Arthur Conan Doyle
- **Stories of Suspense** Nathaniel Hawthorne
- **The Strange Case of Dr Jekyll and Mr Hyde**
  Robert Louis Stevenson
- **Tales of the Supernatural**
- **Three Men in a Boat** Jerome K. Jerome
- **Treasure Island** Robert Louis Stevenson
- **True Adventure Stories** Peter Foreman

READING SHAKESPEARE

- **Julius Caesar**
- **Romeo and Juliet**
- **Twelfth Night**